The Complete Encyclopedia of
Wild Game & Fish Cleaning & Cooking

by Pat Billmeyer

Volume 2 — Small Game

Illustrated Open & Case Skinning, Fleshing, Stretching, Canning, Pickling, Smoking & Freezing

yesnaby publishers

r.d. 8, box 213
danville, pa 17821

Copyright © 1983 by Pat Billmeyer

Published by Yesnaby Publishers, R.D. 8, Box 213, Danville, Pa. 17821

All rights reserved. No part of this book may be reproduced in any manner without written permission from the publisher, except by reviewers who may quote brief passages to be printed in a magazine or newspaper.

Printed and bound in the United States of America.

Library of Congress Catalog Number: 83-50091

International Standard Book Number: 0-9606262-3-9 (Set)
0-9606262-5-5 (Volume)

This book is dedicated to the idea that life is precious. In our lifetime we must take many lives to sustain our own. Each animal we take should be totally utilized - the skin carefully prepared to keep us warm, and the bodies for meat. No child or adult should have their growth or intellect stunted because they waste or do not know how to use the good food God has provided for them.

This SMALL GAME volume tells how to properly skin, flesh and stretch the pelt of each small animal in North America.

It also tells how to clean and cook the small animals, as well as can, pickle, smoke and freeze.

Contents

CHAPTER 1	SMALL GAME CANNING, SALTING, SMOKING & FREEZING	1-4
CHAPTER 2	ARMADILLO General Information...Cleaning...Cooking	5-8
CHAPTER 3	BEAVER General Information...Tracks...Skinning...Cleaning...Cooking	9-15
CHAPTER 4	GROUNDHOG General Information...Tracks...Skinning...Rawhide...Cleaning...Cooking	16-23
CHAPTER 5	RACCOON General Information...Age...Tracks...Skinning...Cleaning...Cooking	23-30
CHAPTER 6	SQUIRREL General Information...Tracks...Skinning...Cleaning...Cooking...Squirrel Heads	31-38
CHAPTER 7	MARMOT General Information...Skinning...Cleaning...Cooking	39-46
CHAPTER 8	MUSKRAT General Information...Tracks...Skinning...	47-55

Cleaning...Cooking

CHAPTER 9   OPOSSUM   56-62
General Information...Tracks...Skinning...
Cleaning...Cooking

**CHAPTER 10   WEASEL, MINK, MARTEN,   63-70
                FISHER, FOX, OTTER, SKUNK,
                LYNX & WILD CAT**
General Information...Skinning...Cleaning

CHAPTER 11   HARE & RABBIT   72-82
General Information...Skinning...Cleaning
...Age...Cooking...Carving

Foreword

All of the recipes in the small game chapter are interchangeable, as long as the animal is properly cleaned and the glands are properly removed. It would be a shame, in my mind, if the excellent curry with fresh orange, which is listed under "Marmot Curry", was only used in the unlikely event you procured a marmot.

I cannot emphasize strongly enough that the cleaning directions under each animal are to be followed exactly. The whole "trick" of cooking small game well lies in the correct removal of certain glands which each animal possesses (and which I have taken some pains to describe).

My husband, Alex Billmeyer II, was my advisor on most skinning and fur preparation. He has not only been a trapper since he was a small boy, he also bought and sold fur for many years.

In case anyone questions the "classiness" of eating wild game, I'd like to start this small game section off with the following menu from the April 18, 1979 meeting of the Explorers Club, which was held at the Waldorf-Astoria in New York City.

EXPLORERS CLUB 75TH ANNUAL DINNER
Exotic Hors d'Oeuvres

Antelope Mousse
Beaver Stew
Buffalo Liver Paté
Wild Boar Hams
Buffalo Meatballs
Roast Loin of Buffalo
Buffalo Steamship Roast
Fried Catfish
Seviche of Codfish Cheeks
Mousse of Elk
Elk Meatballs
Braised Garfish
Hippopotamus Meatballs
Roast Hippopotamus
Quail Eggs in Shell
Civet of Chinese Rabbits
Rattlesnake Chops
Greenland shrimp
Shark Salad
Poached Skate
Roast Shani
Demi Tasse of Witchitty Grub Soup

Small Game Canning, Salting, Smoking & Freezing

Chapter 1

(These directions may be used for all small animals which have been properly cleaned and have the glands removed.)

Make sure the animal has been properly cleaned and THE GLANDS CAREFULLY REMOVED, as directed under each animal. Also, the meat must be FRESH. If it is to be kept over even one day, it must be carefully refrigerated.

Cut the animals into serving sized pieces. Put them in a large pot and cover with boiling water. COVER and simmer slowly for 1/2 to 1 hour, skimming frequently. If there is any excessive foaming or bad odor and there is any suspicion of the meat not being

Small Game

fresh, discard it so neither people or animals can eat it. (This is true when you are canning any kind of meat whatsoever).

If you are using jars, pack in the hot meat loosely, leaving one inch of headroom. Add 1/2 teaspoon salt to pints, 1 teaspoon salt to quarts. Cover with plain, hot water, still leaving 1 inch of headroom. Wipe jar rims perfectly clean and adjust lids. Pressure process at 10 pounds (240 degrees F.) quarts for 75 minutes, pints for 65 minutes. Remove jars; complete seals if necessary.

If you are using plain cans, pack hot meat in loosely, leaving 1/2 inch of headroom. Add 1/2 teaspoon of salt to #2 cans, 3/4 teaspoon salt to #2 1/2 cans. Add clean, boiling water to the top of the cans, leaving no headroom. Wipe can rims carefully to remove drippings. Seal. Pressure-process at 10 pounds (240 degrees F.) - #2 cans for 55 minutes, #2 1/2 cans for 75 minutes. Remove cans and cool quickly.

SERVING THE CANNED MEAT

I am particularly fond of canned meat because it has the delicious taste of a good potroast and it is a fine instant dinner - you have the meat and gravy all ready.

Empty the meat and broth into a pan, combine 2 tablespoons of flour with 4 tablespoons of water until it is smooth, and stir as much of the flour and water mixture as is needed for thickening into the simmering broth. Simmer gently for 3 minutes and serve.

SALTING SMALL GAME

Small game may be preserved by putting into a brine as directed below. They may be kept in the brine until ready for use, in which case they will be very salty and must be put into a kettle of clean water, brought to a boil, simmered for five minutes and then drained, before proceeding with any recipe. This is to remove the excess salt.

Secondly, they may be salted and then smoked as directed below.

PICKLING OR SALT PRESERVING SMALL GAME
Have ready a sterilized crock which is not metal. Combine THOROUGHLY:

6 quarts of water
3 cups pickling salt
1 cup sugar
1 tablespoon saltpeter (Optional. The saltpeter protects the color of the meat, it adds little to the preservation of it.)

After this is thoroughly dissolved, pour it into the crock. This solution will be enough to cover 20 to 30 pounds of game. Add the meat, which has been cleaned as directed, cut into serving sized pieces and washed. MAKE SURE THE GLANDS HAVE BEEN TOTALLY REMOVED AS DIRECTED UNDER EACH ANIMAL.

Put a weighted plate or board over the meat to make sure each piece is held under the brine. If any small piece of the meat sticks out, it can spoil the whole container of meat. Cover it carefully and put it in a cool place where it will stay under 40 degrees.

Every week, remove the cover, turn each piece of meat over, stir the brine carefully and cover. If you ever find the brine has become thick or ropy, remove the meat and scrub each piece, scrub out and scald the container, make new brine and proceed as directed above.

If you are pickling the meat prior to smoking, 15

Small Game

days should be enough for the salt cure before you smoke it.

SMOKING SMALL GAME

I have covered the building of several kinds of smokehouses, etc., very thoroughly in the first book of this series, the "Big Game" section of "The Complete Encyclopedia of Wild Game and Fish Cleaning and Cooking", so I am not going into that again. I will assume that you have your equipment ready.

Since I have advised above that game be cut into serving sized pieces, you will have to run heavy string through each piece and suspend them from the crossrod. I will stick by my decision to cut the game up because the preserving process should be more thorough and shorter.

For small game cut in serving pieces, 48 hours should be enough. If the small game is intact, I would allow 70 hours of smoking.

After it is smoked, it should be wrapped in family-sized portions and put into the freezer. If you do not have a freezer, wrap the pieces individually and put them in airtight containers in a cool place.

FREEZING

Make sure the meat is in meal-sized portions so you don't have to chip away at a giant blob of frozen meat. If you have chops, put a piece of plastic wrap between each so they will separate easily. I always sprinkle meat tenderizer on each piece before wrapping - the tenderizing action accelerates with freezing. Last, use good freezer paper or foil for wrapping and cover tightly so it doesn't get freezer burn.

Armadillo

Chapter 2

Shearn from Florida writes "I must say I was quite shocked when I didn't see a single recipe for Texas Porkers in your book. They are very plentiful here in Florida and I can usually get ten or so with a day's hunting. We grind them up for chili & sausage and also Bar-B-Que, fry and bake them as you would any other small game." Thank you Shearn. Your information is deeply appreciated.

CLEANING THE ARMADILLO
Lay the armadillo on its back and slit the shell lengthwise along its underside. Do not cut through the stomach muscle. Starting at either side, skin the carcass away from the sides of its shell. It pulls away quite easily and it normally takes only a few minutes

Small Game

to skin one.

After skinning, slit the armadillo from vent to neck, then gut. A full grown animal yields from 7 to 10 pounds of a very light pink meat and tastes much like pork.

If anyone can send me information on practical uses for the armadillo shell and signs of his tracks, please be assured it will be appreciated.

ARMADILLO SMOKED BAR-B-QUE

Clean the armadillo as directed above. Cut it into serving sized pieces and wash it in clean water. Drain carefully, put it into a glass bowl and cover it with the following marinade.

Simmer together for 5 minutes:

3 tablespoons oil
1 medium sized chopped onion
2 cloves garlic, crushed with 1/2 teaspoon salt. (Use fork)
1 cup tomato puree or catsup
3 tablespoons brown sugar
1/4 teaspoon brown sugar
Worcestershire or Tabasco sauce to taste (depending on your liking for hotness).

Marinate the meat overnight or longer. Remove the pieces from the marinade and place them in a greased roasting pan and cover tightly. Roast them in a 375 degree F. oven for 1 to 1 1/2 hours, until they are fork tender.

When ready to serve, dip them in the marinade and put them, meat side up, on the grill, 6 to 8 inches above the coals. Brush with marinade and grill for 8 to ten minutes. Brush with marinade again, turn and grill meat side down for about three minutes.

DEVILED ARMADILLO

Clean the armadillo as directed above. Cut it into pieces and put it into a cook pot with a sizable piece of ham. (Use 1/3 as much ham as you have armadillo. An inexpensive piece of ham is ideal for this, including a smoked picnic, ham hock, etc.) Add:

2 cups water
1 or 2 large, chopped onions
1 teaspoon dried parsley, or your favorite herb

COVER tightly and bring to a boil. Skim it and turn the heat down to a gentle simmer for 1 1/2 to 2 hours, until the meat is very tender. Allow it to cool in the broth.

Remove the meat from the broth and bone it, then chop it fine.

Add:

1 cup catsup or tomato barbecue sauce
Salt and Pepper to taste
1 teaspoon to 1 tablespoon ground horseradish (depending on the strength of the horseradish)
1/4 to 2 teaspoons paprika (depending on how devilish you want to get)

Mix this all together and taste for seasoning. Pack this into buttered, glass loaf pans or other deep glass pans. Pour over it clarified butter. (For clarified butter, just heat the butter until it separates from its milky residue, then pour off the butter). If you do not have butter or do not care to spend that much money, pour over it melted lard or any melted shortening instead.

This will keep for quite a while under refrigeration

Small Game

and may be served hot or cold, in sandwiches or as a main course.

Beaver

Chapter 3

The beaver is defined as an amphibious rodent of the genus Castor, valued for its fur, and formerly for a secretion from glands in its groin, used in medicine and perfumery. It is still highly valued for its fur, which is very dense and warm.

TRACKS
The beaver leaves a flatfooted track, and toes in. He covers his forefeet tracks with those of his hind feet. His hind feet are webbed and he has a split toenail on the second toe of his hindfeet. See illustration on next page.

SKINNING THE BEAVER TO SAVE THE FUR
Mr. Robert Betz of R.D. #2, Danville, Pennsylvania, a professional fur trader, has shared with me a rather

Small Game

unique and very efficient way of skinning, fleshing and stretching the beaver hide.

Brush and comb the fur clean of dirt and burrs. Then cut the skin loose around the base of the tail. Now, cut through the skin from the base of the tail to above his abdomen, about 1/3 of the way up the belly. This leaves the upper two thirds of the skin intact to fit firmly over the fleshing beam.

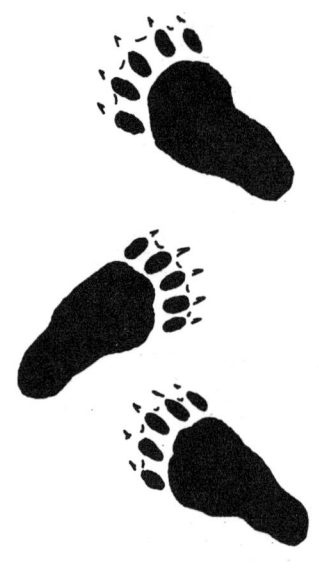

Beaver Tracks

Chapter Three

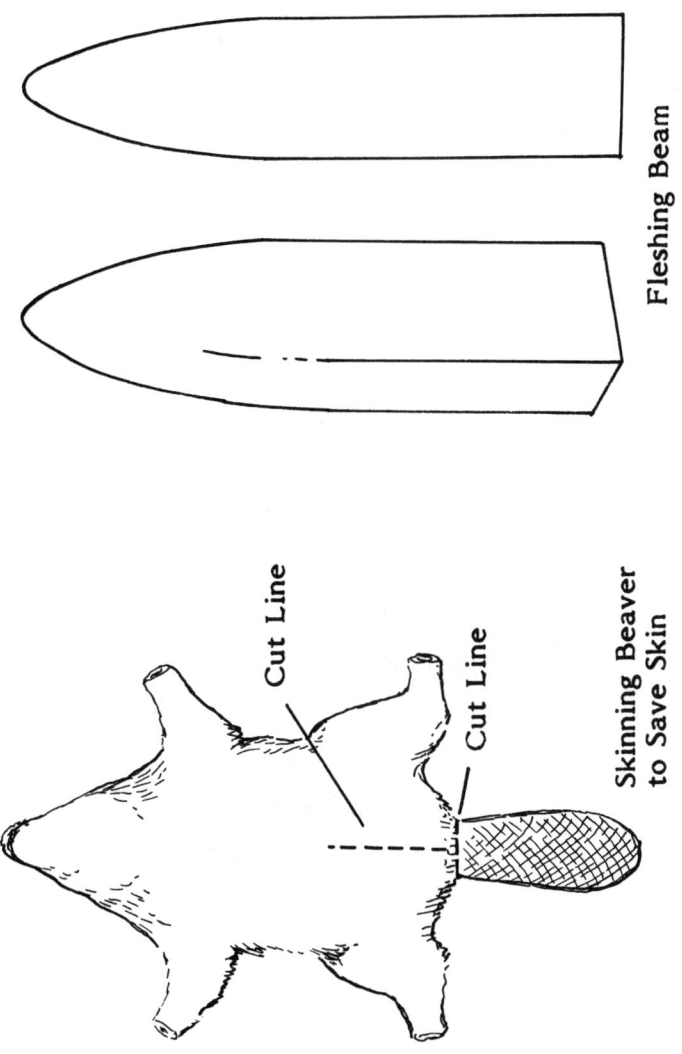

Small Game

Either remove the feet with an axe, or cut the skin in a circle around each ankle. Work the skin loose around the tail, from the tail to the hind legs, and then flay and work loose each hind leg. Now, peel and flay the hide down over the head, cutting through the ear cartilage close to the skull. Skin carefully around the eyes and cut through the nose cartilage, leaving the nose on the hide.

Next, pull the hide, flesh side out over the fleshing beam, with the nose portion over the end of the beam. Holding the fleshing knife almost parallel to the hide, scrape and slice all the fat and excess flesh from the hide, being careful not to pierce the hide. If the fat is not totally removed, it will rot and ruin the value of your fur.

Now, continue your belly cut from the abdomen up under the chin. Put the hide, flesh side out, on the stretcher as soon as it has been fleshed. You will need a piece of plywood 1/2 to 3/4 inches thick and 4 by 4 feet in size. Using #6 finishing nails, nail first the nose, then the tail end, stretched full length, then each side as shown in the illustrations. Since the belly edges of the beaver are apt to be softer, the nails should be put in in the order indicated, not more than an inch apart. Using smaller nails, nail the leg holes shut. See illustration on following page.

Examine the hide and remove any bit of flesh or fat which may have escaped you before. Put the board in a cool, shady place until it is thoroughly dry.

CLEANING

It is important to cut out the castor glands which are located in the groin of the animal. This must be done without piercing the glands because the "castoreum", a yellow secretion, is strong smelling and destroys the taste of the meat. If you are trapping, the

Chapter Three

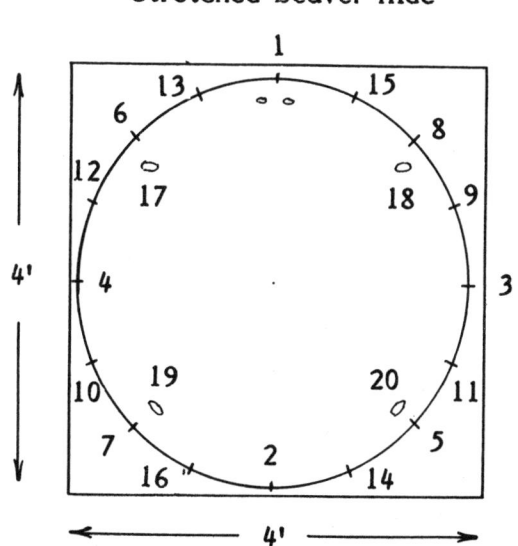

Stretched Beaver Hide

Indians used this secretion on their traps to attract not only the beaver, but other animals.

In any event, remove the glands carefully, slit the carcass from neck to tail and gut. Wash with clear, cold water, inside and outside.

USING THE TAIL

The Indians skinned the tail, turned it inside out, scraped the inside clean and stuffed it carefully with dry leaves and grass, then left it in a cool, shady place to dry. When it was dried they used it as a pouch to carry tobacco, dried corn, etc.

An easy way to eat it is to broil it over hot coals. The skin blisters and comes off in sheets, while the meat underneath roasts beautifullly.

BEAVER TAIL SOUP
1 gallon water

Small Game

1 skinned beaver tail
1 cup chopped onions
1 or 2 fresh garlic cloves, crushed with a fork into 2 teaspoons salt
1 bay leaf
1 teaspoon italian seasoning, or mixed parsley, oregano and thyme
1 large chopped carrot, if you have it

Skin the tail as instructed above. Put the beaver bones and skinned tail into a pot with the water, onions, crushed garlic and salt. If you want to make a richer soup, you can put the whole, cleaned and washed beaver and tail in. Bring this to a boil, then turn down the heat to a steady simmer. Skim the soup and simmer it for one hour. Remove the bones and the tail from the soup, cut the tail up into small cubes and replace the meat in the soup. Add 4 cups of any kind of vegetables you like and have on hand, cut into serving sized pieces. Continue to simmer for another hour, skimming if necessary. Taste for seasoning correction and serve.

BRAISED BEAVER
1 Beaver, cleaned and cut into serving sized pieces
1 cup flour
1 tablespoon salt
1 teaspoon pepper
1/4 to 1/2 cup shortening
1½ cup water
8 carrots
8 small onions
3 cups green or yellow beans

In one 6 quart pressure cooker, bring the shortening to the sizzle. Add the beaver meat which has been tossed in a bag containing the flour, salt and pepper.

Make sure you have pressed the flour mixture firmly into the meat. Brown the meat, turning it carefully so it is browned on all sides.

Pour off the fat and add the water, carrots, onions, beans and 1/2 teaspoon more salt. Cover, set the control on top and cook for 25 minutes after the control jiggles. Cool cooker for five minutes, then place under faucet for 1 minute. Remove control, open and serve.

BEAVER MARENGO
1 Beaver, cleaned as directed above
1/4 cup flour
1 teaspoon salt
1/2 teaspoon pepper
1/2 to 1 cup chopped onion
1 fresh garlic clove, crushed with fork in 1/2 teaspoon of salt
1 cup chicken bouillon or 1 cup water
1/4 to 1/2 cup white or red wine (optional)
1 cup canned or fresh peeled tomatoes
1 bay leaf
1 teaspoon italian seasoning, or 1 teaspoon of mixed dry parsley, oregano and thyme

Put the flour, salt and pepper in a small bag and shake the beaver, which has been cut up into serving sized pieces. Put 1/4 to 1/2 cup butter or other shortening into a heavy pot and bring to the sizzling. Add the floured beaver pieces and brown on all sides. Add the onions and garlic, and brown lightly. Add the water or bouillon, the wine, the tomatoes, the bay leaf and seasoning. Cover tightly and put into a 325 degree oven and bake for 2 to 3 hours, until tender. Add extra liquid, if needed. Serve with buttered noodles or buttered rice.

Groundhog
Chapter 4

(WOODCHUCK, WHISTLE PIG)

These animals do much harm on farms, and any farmer I know (including ourselves), will be glad to get rid of them at any time. Their burrows are feared by farmers because they can upset a tractor. I have seen thirty and forty at a time, out in the fields in Canada.

They are delicious to eat, when properly prepared, because they eat only green, leafy vegetables.

TRACKS

You don't have to wonder whether a woodchuck is around because there's nothing shy about this animal. From about 4 p.m. on, spring through late fall, they congregate in any field where there's anything to eat. Always ask the land owner for permission to hunt, then prepare for good eating.

Chapter Four

SKINNING TO SAVE THE SKIN

It is said that the skin of a groundhog makes excellent rawhide. This is because it is tough. To skin, "case" the animal by cutting along the inside of the hind legs and across the lower abdomen at the vent. Work the skin off the hind legs, cutting off the feet, then pull the skin down, inside out, as you would take off a glove. This will take more muscle than with many animals.

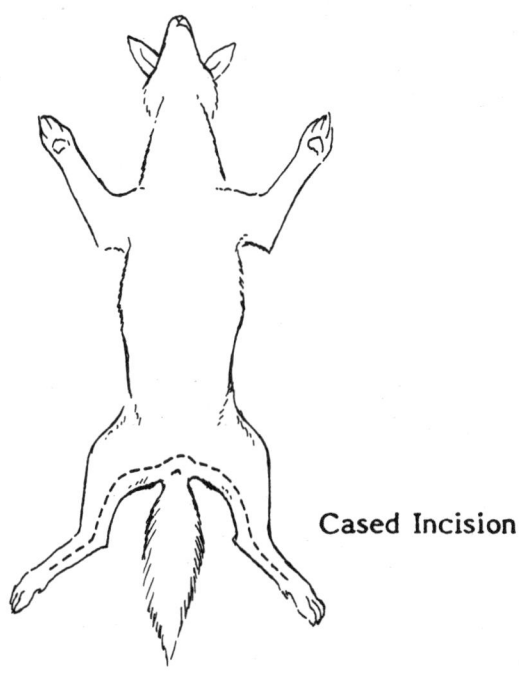

Cased Incision

Now make a wooden stretcher about 30 inches long, 5 inches wide at the shoulders and 8 or 9 inches at the

Small Game

base. My husband always made his stretchers out of wooden shingles which he bought at the lumber yard. He says you can buy ready made wire stretchers but it is a lot more expensive. Make sure the edges are sanded smooth.

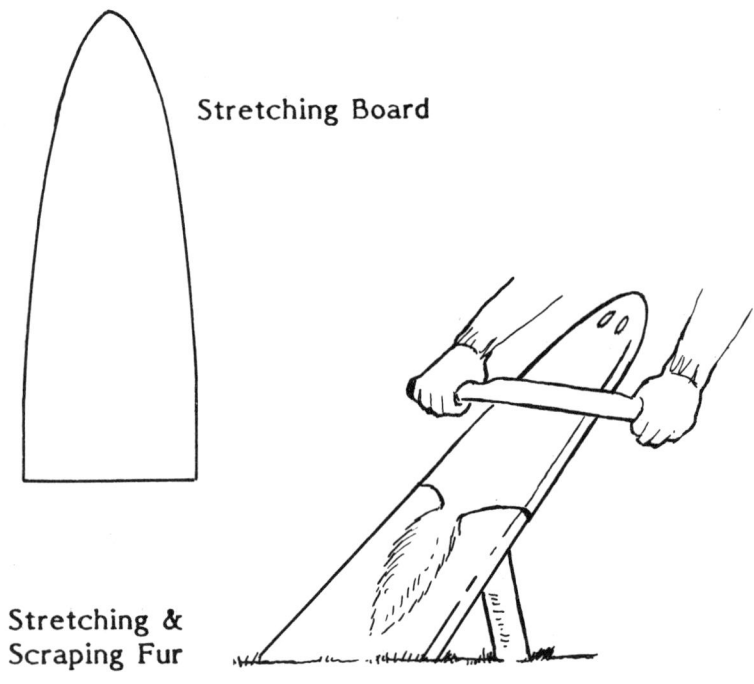

Stretching Board

Stretching & Scraping Fur

If the fur is dirty, wash and dry it before you turn it inside out and work it over the stretcher. Tack it tight, then scrape the inside of the skin clean of all fat and flesh, taking care not to pierce it. Set it, on

Chapter Four

the stretcher, in a cool, shady place where varmints will not bother it.

MAKING RAWHIDE FROM GROUNDHOG SKIN (SEE MY "BIG GAME" BOOK ON TANNING LEATHER AND MAKING RAWHIDE)

When you skin it, don't bother to "case" it. Skin it "open" by slitting the skin from the chin to the anus, then from the slit to the end of each paw.

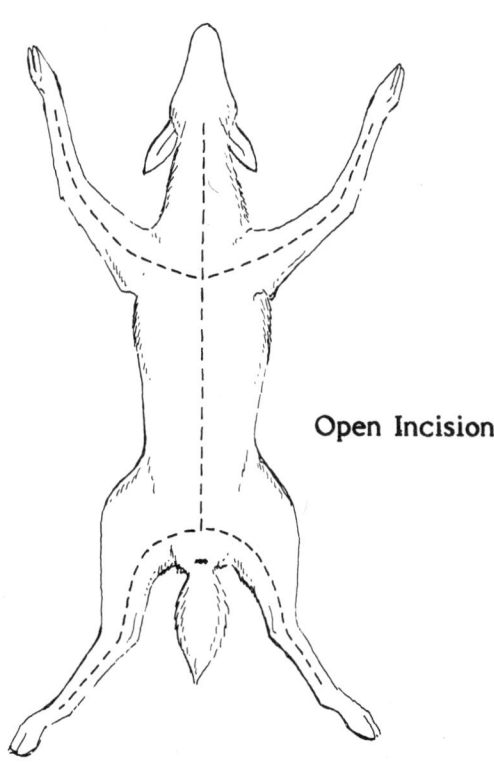

Open Incision

Small Game

Work the fur off of the legs, then the body, and cut off the feet and head. Now scrape off all the flesh and fat on the inside of the skin. Rub wood ashes into the fur and soak, covered in water for several days, until the hair falls out.

Next, stretch the hide tightly on a frame and put it in a cool, shady spot to dry.

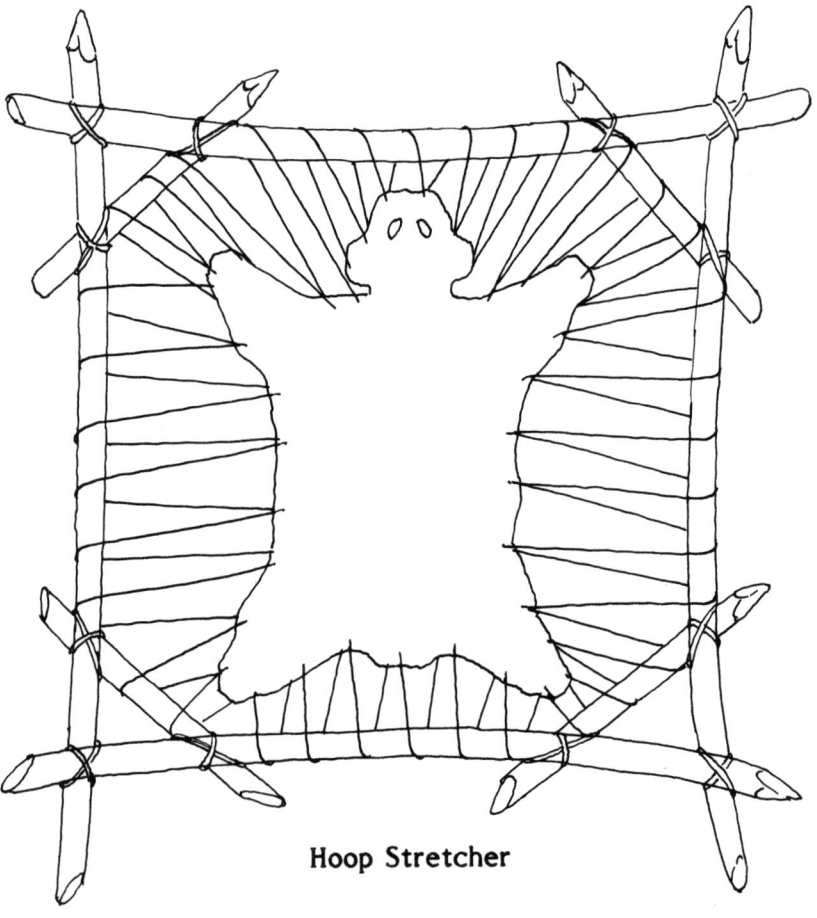

Hoop Stretcher

Chapter Four

When it is dry, rub any good oil (neat's-foot or mineral oil, etc.) into the hide for two or three days in succession. It is now ready to use in making moccasins, rawhide thongs, etc.

SKINNING NOT TO SAVE SKIN
Make sure you have a SHARP knife. Cut the skin entirely around the waist, making sure you do not disturb the glands or kernels in the small of the back. Grab the top part of the skin in one hand and the bottom in the other and pull off to the neck and the feet. Cut off the head, feet and tail. You may need a meat saw, hacksaw or axe for this as the joints and bones are extremely thick. REMOVE THE KERNELS OR NODULES FROM UNDER THE FRONT LEGS AND IN THE SMALL OF THE BACK, WITHOUT CUTTING INTO THEM.

CLEANING
As stated above, the most important thing to remember is to REMOVE THE KERNELS OR GLANDS. Then, slit him from the vent to the neck and remove the guts. Wash out all clots and singe and wash away any remaining hair.

WOODCHUCK OR GROUNDHOG PIE
1 groundhog or woodchuck, prepared as directed above
1½ quarts water
1¼ teaspoons salt
1/2 teaspoon pepper
1/2 cup chopped onion
Herbs (Bay leaf, thyme, italian seasoning as desired)

Put the carcass into a pot with the ingredients listed above. Bring to a boil and barely simmer, COVERED, for 1¼ to 2 hours, until tender, skimming oc-

Small Game

casionally. Let cool. Remove the bones and gristle and dice the meat. Add to the diced meat:
1 to 2 cups diced potatoes
1 to 2 cups mixed vegetables (canned, frozen or fresh)

Boil down the liquid in the pot to about 1½ cups and add the vegetables and meat. Simmer gently for 15 minutes.

Mix 1½ tablespoons of flour with 1/4 cup water until smooth. Add to the simmering mixture and cook another 5 minutes. Pour this into a deep baking dish. Preheat oven to 425° or 450°.

MIX TOGETHER:
1 1/3 cups flour
1 teaspoon salt
POUR INTO ONE MEASURING CUP:
1/3 cup cooking oil
3 tablespoons cold milk

POUR ALL AT ONCE INTO FLOUR. Stir until mixed. Roll it in a ball and put it between 2 pieces of waxed paper and roll it out to fit over your baking dish. Remove the one side of the waxed paper, put the dough over the dish, remove the other piece of waxed paper, flute the sides of the dough and put into the oven for 8 to 10 minutes, until nicely browned. You will probably use this recipe to make pies of all kinds once you try it, as it is the easiest and most foolproof pie pastry recipe I know.

BRAISED GROUNDHOG OR WOODCHUCK

Clean the groundhog as directed above. Cut the animal into serving sized pieces, using a meat saw or cleaver if needed. Combine:

1/2 cup flour

Chapter Four

1 teaspoon salt
1/2 teaspoon pepper

Dredge the groundhog pieces in the flour mixture, pressing it into the meat. Put ¼ cup butter or shortening into a deep, heavy frying pan and brown the pieces of meat evenly on all sides. Pile the browned meat to one side and lightly brown the following in the drippings:

1/2 to 1 cup sliced onions
1 to 2 sliced garlic cloves
Add to the pan:
1 16 oz. can tomatoes or
1 11 oz. can tomato soup or tomato bisque soup
1/2 teaspoon all spice or 1/2 teaspoon cloves
1 teaspoon cinnamon
½ teaspoon salt

COVER and put into a 325 degree oven. Bake 2 to 3 hours, or until fork tender. Add liquid if needed and taste to correct seasoning.

Raccoon

Chapter 5

(COON)
The thing to remember to get a delicious dinner of raccoon is that both the fat and kernels in the small of the back must be removed as they will totally change the good, sweet taste of the meat. There may also be nodules or kernels under the front legs and in the fleshy part of the hind legs. If so, remove them carefully.

AGE OF RACCOON
If the raccoon has old, badly worn teeth, with possibly some broken, he is an oldie and must be braised or preboiled. If he has a full set of sharp teeth, he is younger to middle aged. Look also at size and condition of the animal. If he is young, you will have prize eating ahead of you. At any age, if well prepared, raccoon

is good eating.

RACCOON TRACKS

The raccoon has tracks like a tiny human. He walks flatfooted and has 5 toes on his front and hind feet. He loves sweet corn, as my wrecked garden has attested many times.

Small Game

RACCOON SKINNING IF YOU WANT TO SAVE THE PELT (by all means, do, it is worth a lot of money) The raccoon is skinned "open", as illustrated.

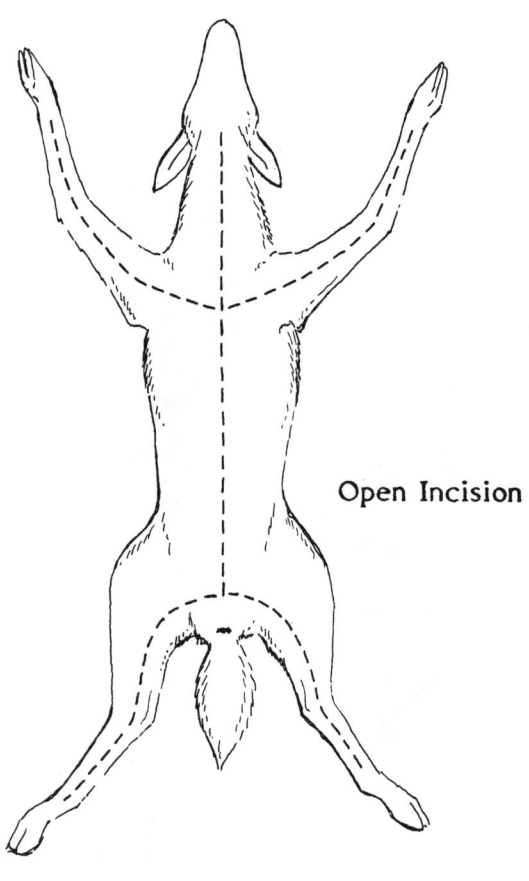

Open Incision

Chapter Five

You cut from the chin, all the way down the stomach to the vent. Then cut from the center slit, down the inside of all four legs. The tail is left attached to the skin, but the bone is removed from the tail and a stick run through it to keep it open for drying. Cut the skin around a ring above the feet and work the skin loose from the hind legs, peel it back from the body, the front legs and over the head, being very careful when cutting around the nose and lips

Make a stretcher about 30 inches long, 10 inches wide at the base and about 6 inches wide at the shoulders as illustrated.

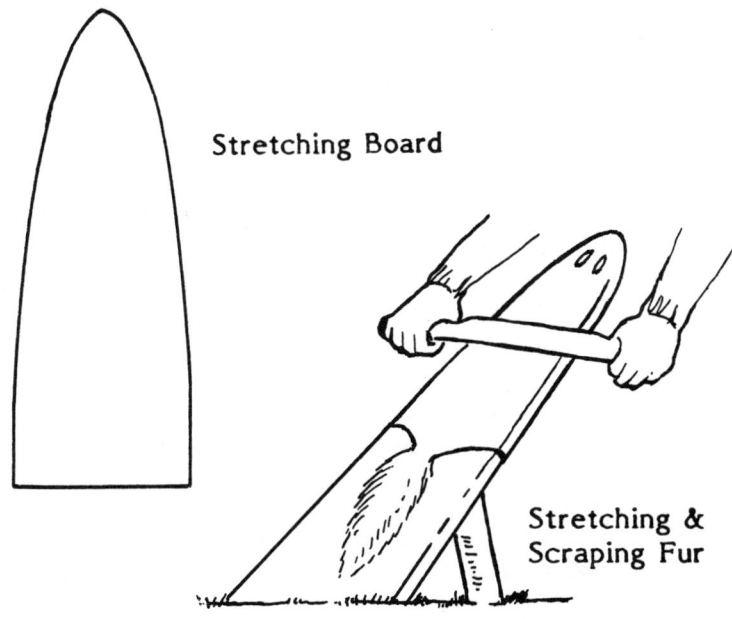

Stretching Board

Stretching & Scraping Fur

Small Game

Tack it carefully on the smooth stretcher, stretching the tail out to full length, with the fur on the inside. "Flesh" the skin carefully, (scrape the excess flesh and fat off) making sure you don't tear the skin. Put it in a shady, cool place to dry.

RACCOON SKINNING IF YOU DON'T SAVE THE HIDE

Cut the skin around the waist of the raccoon, making sure you do not disturb the glands or kernels in the small of the back. Grab the top part of the skin in one hand and the bottom in the other and pull off the skin to the head and to the feet. Cut off the head and tail and feet. Remove the glands or nodules from the small of the back with the point of the knife, making sure you don't pierce them. Check under the front legs and in the fleshy part of the hind legs for kernels or nodules and remove them if you find them. Trim off all fat. Singe the carcass over an open flame if there are any loose hairs sticking to it. Wash thoroughly inside and out, making sure there are no blood clots left in the cavity.

RACCOON CLEANING

Split the raccoon from the anus to the neck and remove the guts. If in the field, clean out the cavity with a little clean grass.

Make sure the kernels or glands in the small of the back, under the front legs and in the fleshy part of the hind legs have been removed. Wash inside and out.

ROAST RACCOON

Gut, skin, degland, defat and wash a raccoon. If he is middle aged or older, put him in a kettle and cover with water. Add:

1 1/2 teaspoons salt

Chapter Five

1 sliced onion
3 cloves, or 1/2 teaspoon crushed cloves
1 teaspoon Italian seasoning or crushed oregano, thyme & parsley

Bring to a boil and simmer COVERED for 1 to 1½ hours, until he is fork tender. If he is very young, you can skip this step. Combine:

1/2 to 1 cup chopped onion
2 or 3 cups cubed bread (depending on the size of the raccoon)
1/2 cup butter or margarine, melted
1/2 teaspoon poultry seasoning or 1 teaspoon mixed herbs
1/2 teaspoon salt
1/2 teaspoon pepper

Taste for seasoning and adjust. Stuff the raccoon and skewer shut the cavity. Put him in a roasting pan surrounded by quartered turnips, parsnips, or other favorite vegetables. Cover him with thinly sliced onions, then bacon strips. Add 1 cup water or broth. COVER and put him in a 400 degree oven for 20 minutes, then 325 degree oven for 1 to 1½ hours, until he is fork tender. Baste frequently.

RACCOON WITH SWEET POTATOES AND PINEAPPLE
Gut, skin, degland, defat and wash the raccoon. Cut him up in serving sized pieces and place in a greased roasting pan. Peel and coarsely dice as many sweet potatoes as you will need to feed your group and lay them around the outside of the meat. Salt the meat and potatoes wih 1 1/2 teaspoons salt and 1/2 teaspoon pepper. Combine:

1 #2 can crushed or diced pineapple

Small Game

3/4 cup brown sugar, firmly packed in measuring cup

Spread this evenly over the raccoon and sweet potatoes. COVER and put into a 325 degree oven for 1½ to 2 hours, until the raccoon is fork tender.

Squirrel

Chapter 6

(SQUIRREL- ARCTIC GROUND, CALIFORNIA GROUND, EASTERN GRAY, PINE, CHICKEREE, FOX, RED, RICHARDSON'S GROUND, ROCK, WESTERN GRAY, TASSEL EARED, KAIBAB, ALBERT)

All squirrels are edible, but many are too small to make more than a bite. The gray squirrel and the fox squirrel are most commonly eaten. At any rate, the decision is yours. If it's big enough, it will make a delicious meal.

SQUIRREL TRACKS
The tiny track of the forefeet are BEHIND the hind feet. Sometimes there is a trace of his long tail. See illustration on next page.

Small Game

Squirrel Tracks

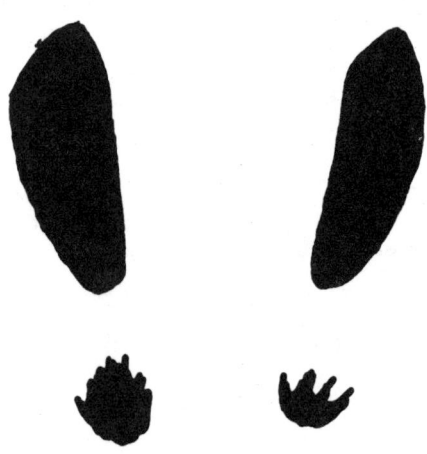

SQUIRREL SKINNING TO SAVE THE FUR

Most of the fur for squirrel coats in this country is imported. Since we have definite hunting seasons for squirrel, and limits on the amounts that can be taken, we cannot produce enough to supply the market. If we did not restrict the hunting of squirrel, we would not have any left alive, for I know what the hunting season does to our squirrel population. This is all the more reason to use the skin as well as the meat. We must be good stewards.

A squirrel should be "cased" and his fur put on a stretcher. The stretcher should be about 12 inches long and four inches wide at the base. Make sure the edges of the stretcher are rounded and smooth.

Chapter Six

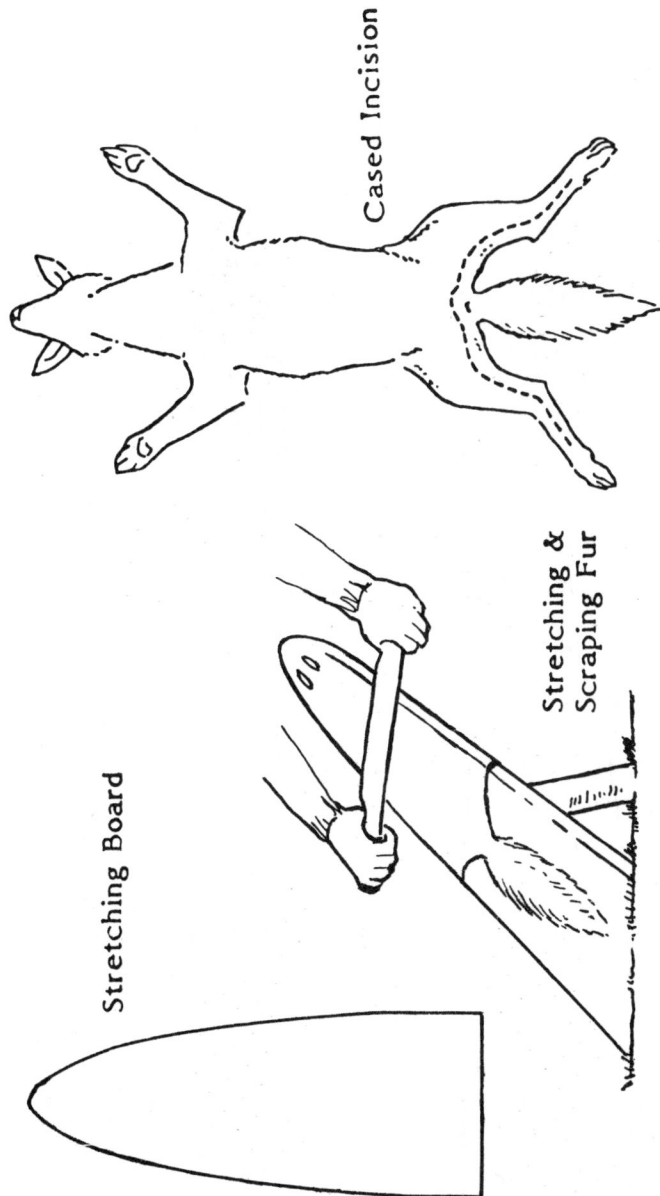

Small Game

To "case", cut along the inside of both hind legs and across the vent. Skin out the hind legs. Cut a circle around the skin at the ankle and work out the legs. The tail is to be left on the hide - pull the bones out of the tail and run a stick through it so the air can enter. Pull the skin inside out, down over the animal, as you would remove a glove. Cut a circle around the skin at the front ankles and work out the legs. Peel the pelt over the head, taking great care when you skin out around the eyes and lips, so you don't pierce the skin.

Stretch the fur over the stretcher with the fur inside and tack the skin smooth. Be sure you stretch and tack the tail. Scrape the flesh and fat off the hide carefully. You will get more money for the pelt if this is done thoroughly.

Put in a cool, airy place to dry.

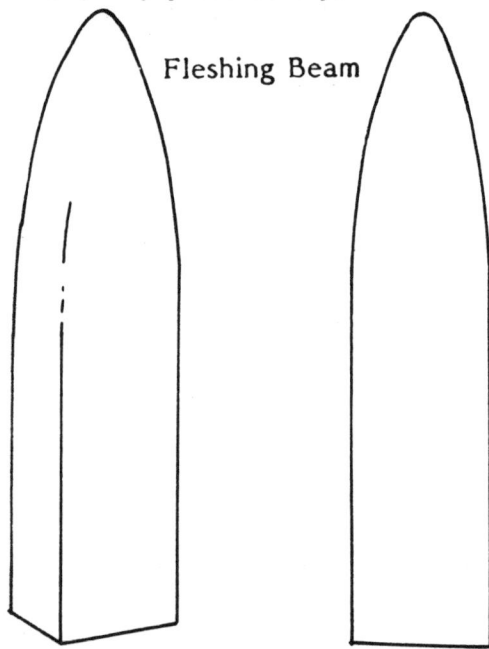

Fleshing Beam

Chapter Six

SQUIRREL SKINNING IF YOU DON'T WANT TO SAVE THE SKIN
Cut the skin of a squirrel clear around the midsection, and pull both ways. The squirrel head is considered a delicacy in many homes and if you want to cook it as directed at the end of the chapter, skin the head too, then cut it off. If you don't want to eat the head, cut the body off at the neck before skinning. Now, over an open flame, singe off any hair sticking to the carcass. Wash thoroughly, inside and out, making sure all blood and clots are removed from the body cavity.

SQUIRREL CLEANING OR GUTTING
All squirrels should be gutted immediately in the field. Split the squirrel from neck to vent and remove guts. Wipe out with a little clean grass.

FRIED SQUIRREL
(My mother's recipe and her mother's before her)
Gut, skin, singe and wash squirrel as directed above. Cut it into quarters and place in a deep kettle. Cover with water and add:

1 chopped onion
1 large chopped carrot
1 stalk chopped celery
1 teaspoon salt
1 bay leaf

Simmer for one hour, or until it is fork tender. Drain. Combine:
1/2 cup flour
1 teaspoon salt
1/2 teaspoon pepper

Small Game

Press the squirrel pieces into this mixture. Put 1/4 to 1/2 cup butter, margarine or bacon drippings into a fry pan and bring to a sizzle. Brown the squirrel carefully on all sides. Remove to a platter. Add to the drippings:

1 tablespoon flour
1/2 teaspoon garlic salt
1 tablespoon onion juice or 1 small chopped onion
1/2 teaspoon italian seasoning or mixed thyme, oregano & parsley
Accent, if needed
1 cup canned chicken bouillon, or 1 cup water

Stir with a wire wisk or egg beater until smooth and simmer gently for 3 to 5 minutes. Serve with the squirrel.

SQUIRREL STEW
Gut, skin, singe and wash squirrel as directed and cut into quarters. Put into a kettle with:

1 quart water
1 teaspoon salt
1 large chopped onion
2 chopped carrots
1/4 teaspoon pepper
2 tablespoons wine, gin or lemon juice
1 bay leaf
1 teaspoon italian seasoning or mixed herbs

Bring to a boil, then turn down to the simmer and skim. Simmer gently for 1 to two hours, until fork tender, skimming if necessary. Remove the squirrel quarters from the pot, allow to cool and remove the bones.

Put them back into the broth with:

1 16 ounce can of tomatoes
1 16 ounce can lima beans

Bring to the boil, then turn down to a simmer for 1/2 hour. Add:

1 16 ounce can creamed corn
1 cup mashed potatoes

Stir and simmer this for 15 minutes, making sure it doesn't burn. Correct seasoning. Serve with hot corn bread.

SQUIRREL HEADS
Skin the heads as directed under "squirrel skinning". Remove the eyes and ears. Cover them with cold water to which one tablespoon of salt has been added and soak in the refrigerator for at least 12 hours. Drain and wash again. Put them in a kettle and cover with water to which you add:

1 teaspoon salt
1 chopped onion
1 chopped carrot
1 bay leaf
1 teaspoon mixed herbs
2 slices lemon

Bring to a boil, COVER and simmer gently for one hour. Drain and dry. Put in a frying pan 1/4 to 1/2 cup butter, margarine or bacon drippings and bring to a sizzle. Add 1 cup thinly sliced onions and the squirrel heads. Brown the onions and squirrel heads lightly, shaking the pan to turn them. You may add 1/4 cup wine

Small Game

or beef bouillon to the pan drippings. Bring this to a boil, stirring with a wire wisk. Pour over the squirrel heads and onions. The jowls, tongue and brains are considered great delicacies.

Marmot

Chapter 7

(HOARY MARMOT) (WHISTLER OF THE ROCKIES)
　　He is a bush-tailed, thick-set rodent running 27 to 28 inches at maturity.
　　The white tips on its black fur give a hoary or frostlike appearance to this animal and account for its name. It is related to the North American Prairie dog and the Woodchuck and its method of cleaning and cooking are really interchangeable.

Small Game

MARMOT OR HOARY MARMOT SKINNING IF YOU WANT TO KEEP THE FUR

The Indians valued the fur of the marmot very highly, because it is both beautiful and tough. It can be either skinned "open" or "cased". If skinned "open", follow this illustration.

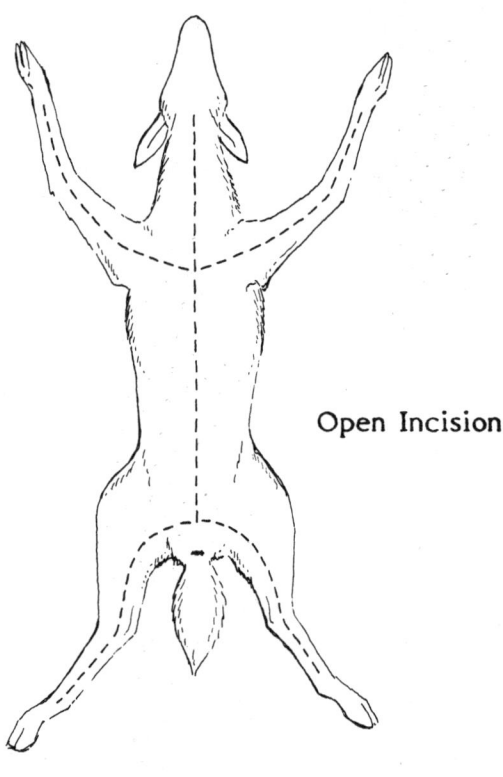

Open Incision

Chapter Seven

Cut the hide from the chin, to the vent. Now cut from center slit, out the inside of all four legs to the paws. If you do not want the feet, cut them off. Put the hide on a "hoop" stretcher.

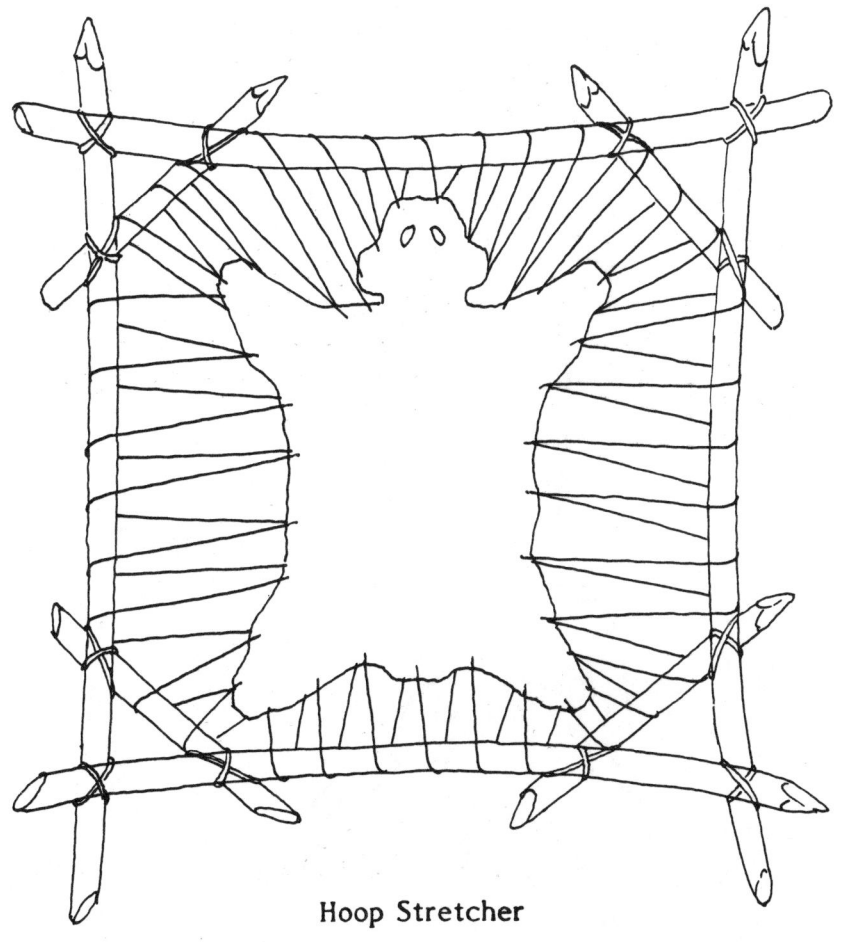

Hoop Stretcher

Small Game

If you want to "case" it, cut along the inside of the hind legs and across the vent, as illustrated.

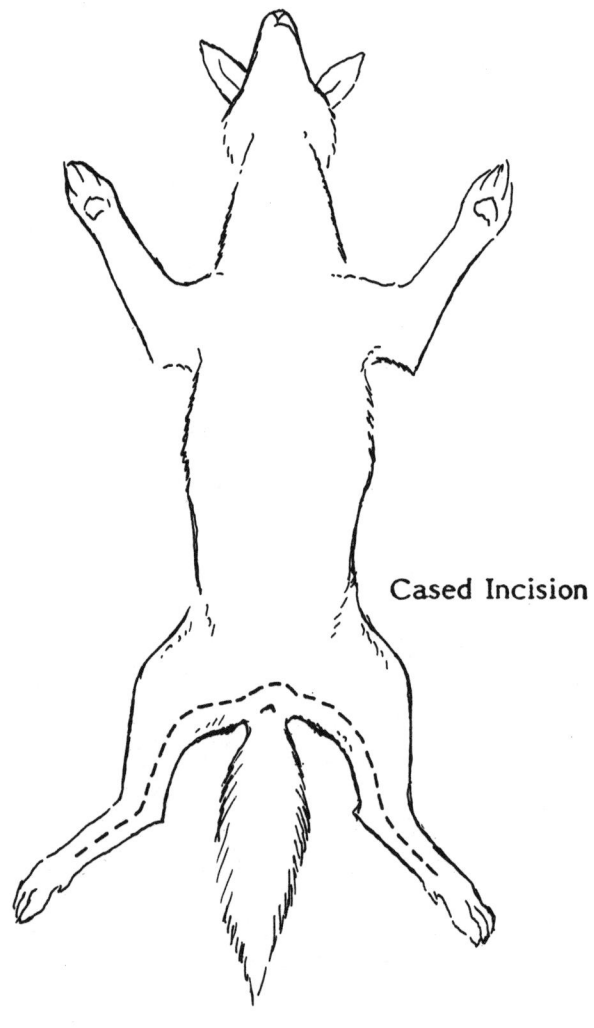

Cased Incision

Chapter Seven

Pull out the bones inside the tail and clean the area out with a stick. Make a stretcher as illustrated, thirty inches long, 6 inches wide at shoulders and 8 to 10 inches wide at base. Make sure all the edges are sanded smooth. My husband always made his out of roof shingles which he got at the lumber yard. He says they are cheap and convenient.

If the fur is dirty, wash it off but make sure it's dry before you stretch it on the stretcher. Pull it over the stretcher fur side in, and stretch it carefully until it is smoothly stretched to its full length and width. Stretch the hind legs and tail full length. Scrape off excess flesh or fat and put in a cool, shady place to dry, away from varmints.

MARMOT OR HOARY MARMOT SKINNING IF YOU DON'T WANT THE HIDE

They have the hide of a rhinoceros so you'll need a sharp knife. Cut the skin entirely around the waist, making sure you do not disturb the glands or kernels in the small of the back. Grab the top part of the skin in one hand and the bottom in the other and pull off the neck and the feet. Cut off the head, feet and tail. You may need a meat or hacksaw for this as the joints and bones are extremely thick.

MARMOT CLEANING OR GUTTING

Slit the marmot from the anus to the neck and remove the guts. If in the field, clean out the cavity with a little clean grass.

Remove the kernels or nodules from under the front legs and in the small of the back. Trim off all fat. Singe the carcass over an open flame if there are any loose hairs sticking to it. Wash thoroughly inside and out, making sure there are no blood clots left in the cavity.

Small Game

MARINATED MARMOT
1 marmot, cleaned as directed above
1/2 cup oil
1/8 cup burgundy wine or, if a teetotaler, 1/8 cup cider vinegar
1 teaspoon salt (Onion salt, if you have it)
1/2 teaspoon pepper
1 sliced clove garlic (2 if you love it)
1 tablespoon brown sugar

Cut the marmot into serving sized pieces, put it in a glass dish or bowl and cover it with the above marinade. If it doesn't quite cover it, add 1/2 cup of water. Marinate overnight to 48 hours, turning about every eight hours.

Drain and dry the meat, reserving the marinade. Mix:

1/2 cup flour
1 teaspoon salt
1/4 teaspoon pepper
1/4 to 1/2 teaspoon curry powder

Press the pieces of marmot into this mixture. Heat to the sizzling 1/4 cup butter or margarine and brown the floured marmot on all sides. Pour in the marinade, COVER and put in a 325 degree oven for 2 hours, or until fork tender. Add more liquid only if it is needed.

MARMOT BAKED WITH APPLES
Clean and wash the marmot as directed above. Mix together:

1 cup flour
1 teaspoon salt
1/4 teaspoon pepper

Chapter Seven

Press this flour mixture into the marmot. Bring to the sizzling 1/2 cup butter, margarine or bacon drippings and brown the floured marmot on all sides. Put the browned marmot in a buttered roasting pan or baking dish and add 3 apples, peeled and cut in eighths. Pour over the pan drippings. Cover closely with brown sugar and sprinkle with cinnamon. Add 1 cup chicken broth.

Bake in 325 degree oven for 1½ to 2 hours, until fork tender. Add more liquid if needed. Taste for seasoning and serve.

MARMOT PREPARATION FOR CURRY, MEAT PIES, ETC.
Put the marmot into a kettle and add:

1½ quarts water
1½ teaspoons salt
1 teaspoon italian seasoning or 1 teaspoon mixture oregano, thyme and parsley
1 or two chopped onions

COVER, bring to a boil and simmer, skimming occasionally, about 1½ to 2 hours, until fork tender. Cool, drain and remove the bones. Continue with the following recipes.

MARMOT CURRY
Marmot prepared as directed above.

3 tablespoons butter or margarine
1/2 cup chopped onion
2 tablespoons flour
1 to 2 teaspoons curry powder (depending on how "hot" you want it)

Small Game

1/2 teaspoon salt
1½ cups chicken stock (if canned, undiluted)
1 orange, quartered, skin and all

In a large frying pan, bring the butter to the sizzle. Add the onion and cook, gently, until it is starting to turn brown. Sprinkle over it the flour, the curry powder and the salt. Stir and cook this until it is well blended, then add 1½ cups chicken stock, stirring vigorously. Bring it to the boil, turn down the heat and barely simmer it for 5 minutes. Add the prepared marmot meat and 1 orange, quartered, skin and all. Crush the orange into the sauce and cook gently, crushing the orange, for another 5 minutes. Remove what is left of the orange quarters, taste for seasoning and serve with rice.

STOVIES

When I first went to an English pub and was offered "stovies" I couldn't imagine what they were, but I tried them out of curiosity. I have tried to reconstruct it here, but I cannot say I will be held accountable by a "stovie" purist. It is a tasty, quick dish which uses up leftover mashed potatoes and constitutes a complete, if fattening, lunch.

4 tablespoons butter, margarine or other shortening
1/2 cup sliced onion
1 to 2 cups marmot meat prepared as directed above
   (Their "stovies", of course, were not made with marmot but were probably beef or pork.)
1 to 3 cups mashed potatoes

Stir all together and brown gently. Taste for seasoning and serve.

Muskrat

Chapter 8

MUSKRAT (MARSH RABBIT)
   This is one of the most clean living and clean animals known to man and the taste of the meat reflects its habits. Its meat is almost always wasted, which is a terrible shame, because it is trapped primarily for its fur.
   Please consult the small game canning directions at the beginning of the book. During trapping season, many muskrat are taken at one time, and it is a great SHAME to waste the meat. Every day the fresh meat should be properly cleaned as directed and canned or frozen. The family would save a tremendous amount of money for the rest of the year.
   The greatest care must be taken to remove the glands or kernels under the front legs and in the small of the back for they will destroy the sweet, good taste of the meat.

MUSKRAT TRACKS
   The muskrat track is flatfooted, with toes pointing

Small Game

nearly straight ahead. Four toes are on his front feet, five on his hind feet. In between his footprints is a wavy line made by his ratlike tail.

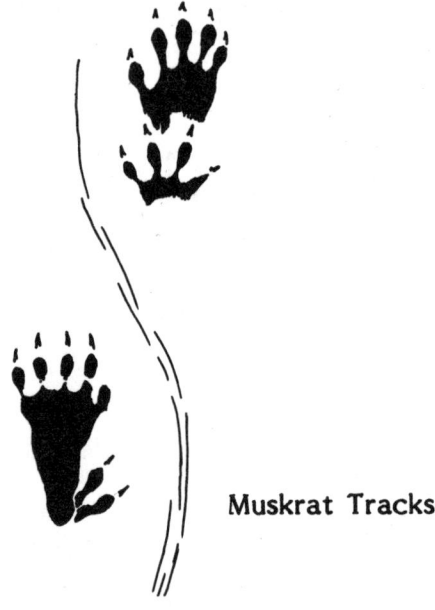

Muskrat Tracks

SKINNING THE MUSKRAT TO SAVE ITS FUR (A great extra source of income for many people.)

The muskrat skin is "cased", which means to cut along the inside of the hind legs and across the bottom as shown in the illustration on the next page.

After slitting the skin as indicated, skin out the hind legs. Cut a ring around the ankle and pull the skin off the legs. Cut the skin around the tail. The tail stays on the carcass and can be used as a handle. Continue to pull the skin off the animal as you would remove a glove, work out the front legs and cut the skin in a ring around the ankle and remove from the front legs. Peel the skin over the head. Cut the ears close to

Chapter Eight

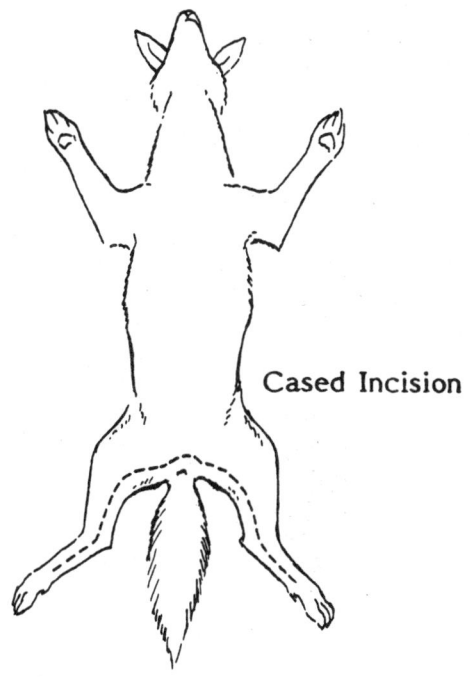

Cased Incision

the flesh so you don't cut the skin. Continue to peel off the skin, taking great care in cutting around the eyes and lips, so the head skin comes off in one piece, without being cut or torn.

Have ready a "stretcher". My husband always made a stretcher from wood shingles which he bought at the lumber yard. Any wooden board 1/2 to 3/4 inch thick will do. For the muskrat it must be about 20" long, 5" wide at the shoulders and 7" or 8" wide at the base.

Small Game

All of the edges must be round and smooth. Pull the fur over the stretcher fur side in. Tack the nose and lips in position, and pull the skin down to its full length and tack the end. Place sticks in the forelegs to stretch them out, and tack the hind legs full length.

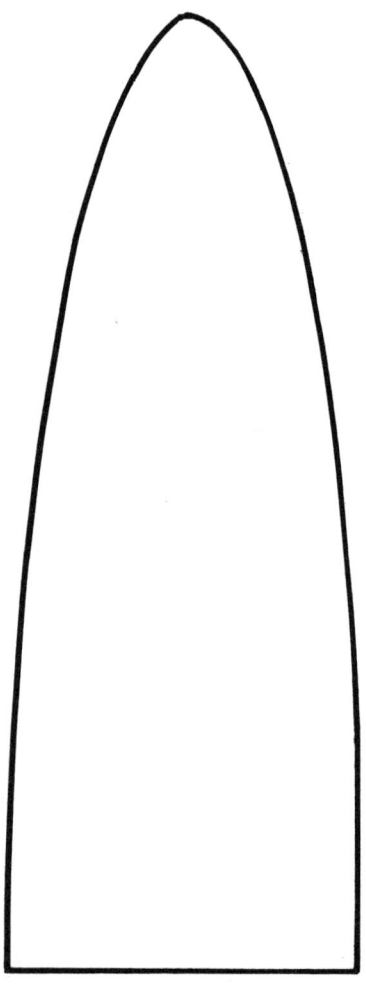

Chapter Eight

Now scrape or "flesh" your fur carefully. Scrape CAREFULLY with the edge of a good sharp knife, being super careful not to cut into the pelt, or you've lost a lot of money value on your fur. The more carefully your pelt is "fleshed", the higher price you will get for your fur.

Stretching & Scraping Fur

Small Game

Put it to dry in a cool, shady place, where the air can flow freely around it. If you want to tan the hide yourself, consult my first book in this series, the "BIG GAME" section of "THE COMPLETE ENCYCLOPEDIA OF WILD GAME & FISH CLEANING AND COOKING".

SKINNING THE MUSKRAT IF YOU DON'T WANT THE PELT

If you are only interested in eating, cut the skin entirely around the middle, making sure you don't pierce the glands in the small of the back. Loosen a little of the skin and grab the top part in one hand and the bottom part in the other and pull off the skin. Cut off the head, feet and tail.

MUSKRAT CLEANING

Slit the muskrat from the vent to the neck and remove the guts. With the tip of your knife, REMOVE THE GLANDS OR KERNELS IN THE SMALL OF THE BACK AND UNDER THE FORELEGS. Cut far enough around them so you will not pierce them and spoil the flesh.

If there is hair clinging to the carcass, singe it off over an open flame. Wash the muskrat carefully inside and out, making sure all blood clots are removed from the cavity. Soak overnight in salted water, using 1 tablespoon of salt to 1 quart of water. Drain, rinse and proceed.

MUSKRAT CREOLE

Cut, skin, degland, wash and presoak the muskrat as directed above. Cut in serving pieces. Cover him with clean water to which you have added:

1/2 cup sliced onion
1 sliced carrot

1 bay leaf
1 teaspoon Italian seasoning or mixed oregano, thyme and parsley
1 teaspoon salt
1 teaspoon lemon juice or several slices of lemon with peel

Bring this to a boil and simmer it until it is fork tender, about 1½ hours. Drain. Combine:

1 teaspoon salt
1/2 teaspoon pepper
1/2 cup flour

Press each piece into this mixture until well coated. Put them in a pan which contains 1/2 cup sizzling butter, margarine, or bacon drippings. Brown them evenly. Add to the pan:

1 cup sliced onion
1/2 to 1 cup sliced green peppers or mangoes, as the Dutch call them
2 cups peeled tomatoes or 1 16 oz. can of tomatoes
1 teaspoon Worcestershire sauce
1 tablespoon soy sauce
2 tablespoons brown sugar
1 teaspoon paprika

COVER and put in 325 degree oven. Bake for 1 hour. Taste to correct seasoning and serve.

MUSKRAT WITH GIN
Gin, made fom the juniper berry, tenderizes and gently flavors the meat. Gut, skin, degland, wash and presoak muskrat as directed. Drain and dry him with paper towels. Rub the muskrat inside and out with gin,

Small Game

salt and pepper. Then make the following stuffing:

2 apples, chopped
2 cups bread crumbs
1/2 cup raisins or chopped, pitted prunes
½ teaspoon salt
½ teaspoon mace
3 tablespoons brown sugar
1/2 cup melted butter or margarine

Combine the above ingredients lightly with a fork and taste for seasoning. Stuff it into the muskrat and skewer shut the cavity. Put the muskrat into a roasting pan and pour over it 1/4 to 1/2 cup gin. (Depending on the size of the muskrat.) Add 1 cup of undiluted canned chicken bouillon. COVER and put in a 325 degree oven. Bake for 1½ to 2 hours, until tender, basting with the juices every half hour. Add more gin and bouillon if needed.

FRIED MUSKRAT

This is the way my mother served muskrat and it is simple and delicious.

Cut, skin, degland and soak the muskrat as directed above. Drain and wash. Put him in a pot, cut into serving sized pieces, and add:

1 teaspoon salt
1/4 teaspoon pepper
1 to 2 quarts water (to cover)
1 sliced onion
1 teaspoon lemon juice or 2 slices fresh lemon, peel and all

COVER and simmer gently until he is fork tender. Drain and cool.

Chapter Eight

When you are about 45 minutes from dinner, get 1/4 to 1/2 cup butter, margarine or bacon drippings sizzling gently in a frying pan. Combine:

1/2 cup flour (1 cup if it's a big muskrat)
1/2 to 1 teaspoon salt
1/4 teaspoon pepper

Coat the pieces carefully with this mixture, pressing it in. Put it into the frypan and brown the pieces on all sides. Push them to one side and add one cup of sliced onions. COVER and turn down the heat so it fries very gently for 1/2 hour. Take off the cover and turn the meat. Fry it gently for 2 or 3 more minutes and serve.

Opossum

Chapter 9

(POSSUM, VIRGINIA OPOSSUM)
The opossum is defined as a prehensile-tailed, pouched marsupial mammal, the size of a large cat, which feigns death when caught. That just about covers it, except that it has always fascinated me that a new born opossum is the size of a kidney bean. A teaspoon can hold 15 to 18 newborn opossums.

OPOSSUM TRACKS
The opossum tracks are weird and unmistakable because his hind feet have a thumb. He has 5 toes on front and hind feet with claws on all toes except the thumbs.

Chapter Nine

Opossum Tracks

SKINNING OPOSSUM IF YOU WANT TO SELL THE HIDE

The opossum hide is not as valuable as some other furs, because he has long guard hairs but a very poor undercoat. However, his value is certainly high enough to make it worthwhile skinning and stretching the hide.

The opossum skin is "cased", which means to cut along the inside of the hind legs and across the bottom as shown in the illustration on the next page.

After slitting the skin as indicated, skin out the hind legs. Cut a ring around the ankle and pull the skin off the legs. Cut the skin around the tail. The tail stays on the carcass and can be used as a handle. Continue to pull the skin off the animal as you would remove a glove, work out the front legs and cut the skin in a ring around the ankle and remove from the front

Small Game

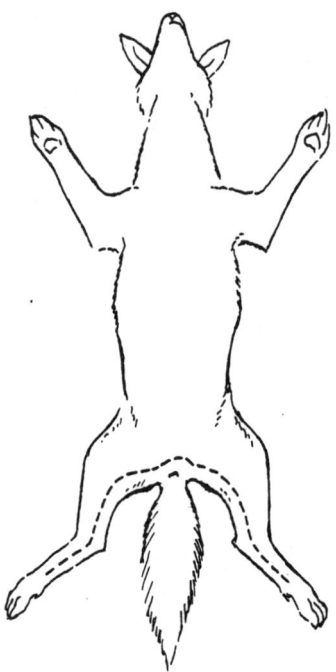

Cased Incision

legs. Peel the skin over the head. Cut the ears close to the flesh so you don't cut the skin. Continue to peel off the skin, taking great care in cutting around the eyes and lips, so the head skin come off in one piece, without being cut or torn.

Have ready a "stretcher". My husband made stretchers from wood shingles from the lumber yard. Any wooden board 1/2 to 3/4 inch thick will do. For the opossum the board should measure 28 to 30 inches long, 8 inches wide at the base and 5 or 6 inches wide at the shoulder. All edges must be smooth. Pull the fur

Chapter Nine

over the stretcher fur side in. Tack the nose and lips in position, and pull the skin down to its full length and tack the end. Place sticks in the forelegs to stretch them out, and tack the hind legs full length.

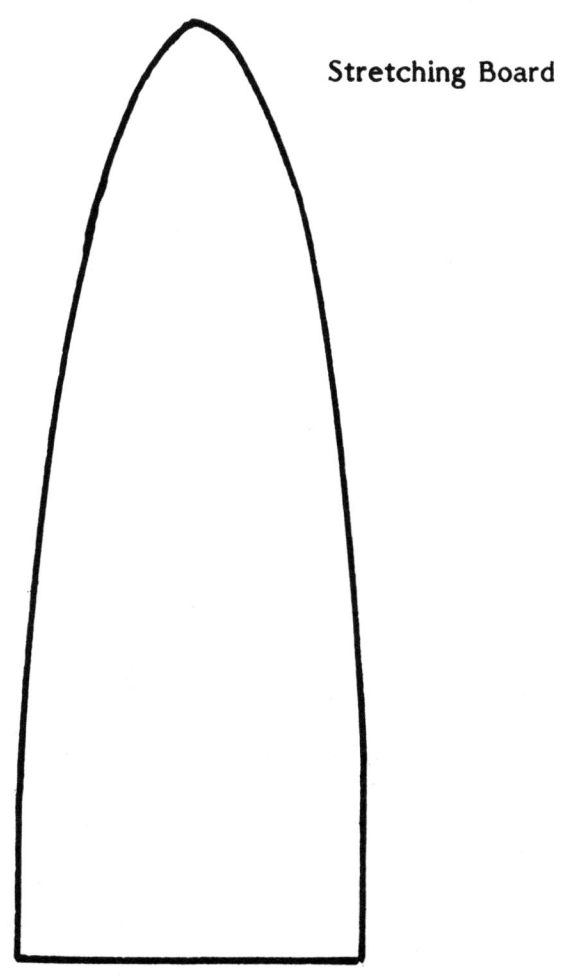

Stretching Board

Small Game

Now scrape or "flesh" your fur carefully. Scrape CAREFULLY with the edge of a good sharp knife, being super careful not to cut into the pelt.

Put it to dry in a cool, shady place, where the air can flow freely around it.

Stretching & Scraping Fur

Chapter Nine

SKINNING OPOSSUM IF YOU DON'T WANT TO SAVE THE HIDE

Cut the skin entirely around the middle, making sure you don't pierce the glands in the small of the back. Loosen a little of the skin and grab the top part in one hand and the bottom part in the other and pull off the skin. Cut off the head, feet and tail.

CLEANING OPOSSUM

Slit the opossum from the vent to the neck and remove the guts. If you are in the field, wipe out the cavity with clean grass. After skinning, take the tip of your knife and remove the kernels or glands in the small of the back and under the forelegs. Give the glands plenty of room so you don't cut into them, or they will spoil your meat. If there is hair clinging to the carcass, singe it off over an open flame. Wash it carefully, inside and out, making sure all blood clots are removed from the cavity.

ROAST OPOSSUM WITH SAUSAGE DRESSING

Skin, clean and degland the opossum as directed above. Wrap him lightly in waxed paper and put him in the meat keeper for 24 to 48 hours. Cover him with water, add 1/4 cup salt to the water and let him soak for 12 hours. Drain and rinse. Combine:

1 cup sausage meat
1/2 cup chopped onion
2 to 3 cups diced bread, depending on the size of the opossum
1/2 teaspoon salt
1/2 teaspoon pepper
1 teaspoon Italian seasoning or mixed herbs

Small Game

The chopped opossum liver

Stuff the opossum and skewer shut the opening. Put him in a roasting pan with:

2 cups water
1 large chopped onion
1 large bay leaf
1 teaspoon salt
1/2 cup chopped celery

COVER and put in 425 degree oven for 15 minutes. Turn it down to 325 degrees and roast 1 1/2 to 2 1/2 hours, until fork tender.

OPOSSUM BAKED WITH SWEET POTATOES AND ORANGES

Skin, clean and degland opossum as directed above. Wrap him lightly in waxed paper and put into the meat keeper for 24 to 48 hours. Cut into serving sized pieces and put into a bowl and cover with water. Add 1/4 to 1/2 cup salt. Stir until dissolved, cover and soak for 12 hours more. Drain and wash the meat carefully. Put the pieces in a roasting pan and surround the meat with peeled sweet potatoes cut in pieces. Sprinkle 1½ teaspoons of salt over the sweet potatoes and meat. Thinly slice 2 unpeeled oranges and cover the potatoes and meat thickly. (Use orange number three if needed.) Sprinkle over the oranges 3/4 cup tightly packed brown sugar or 3/4 cup honey. COVER and bake in 325 degree oven for two hours, or until fork tender.

Weasel, Mink, Marten, Fisher, Fox, Otter, Skunk, Lynx & Wild Cat

Chapter 10

These animals are almost always taken for their fur. They are all "cased", fleshed and stretched on stretching boards. Because I am running out of space, I am going to give "casing", stretching and fleshing instructions once, at the beginning of this chapter. Individual variations, such as the size of the stretchers, will be noted under each animal.

Also included under each animal will be variations of the cleaning process; namely, individual gland removal. Each animal can be canned, pickled, smoked, etc., as in the instructions given at the beginning of this small game volume. Also, all recipes given for any small game can be used interchangeably, as long as THE GLANDS HAVE BEEN REMOVED.

Which brings me to the biggest problem I have had during the seven years I have been researching and

Small Game

writing this book - where are the glands of the individual animals located which must be removed before cooking? At one point, I even contacted the United States Army and the United States Air Force Survival School. (They never answered). I have finally gotten the information for all except the few which will be indicated. If anyone out there has any information on these omissions, please write to me.

If you want to go one step further and tan the hides, complete directions are contained in Volume 1 of this series, "Big Game" of "The Complete Encyclopedia of Wild Game and Fish Cleaning and Cooking."

TO "CASE" SKIN AN ANIMAL

To "case", cut the skin along the inside of both hind legs and across the vent, as illustrated. Skin out the hind legs. Cut a circle around the skin at the ankle and work out the legs. The tail is to be left on the hide - pull the bone out of the tail and run a stick through it so the air can enter. Pull the skin inside out, down over the animal, as you would remove a glove. Cut a circle around the skin at the front ankles and work out the legs. Peel the pelt over the head, taking great care when you skin out around the eyes and lips, so you don't pierce the hide. See illustration on following page.

If you are going to skin many animals it would pay you to have a fleshing "beam" which is simply a wooden beam set on end, with one end pointed and sanded round and smooth, over which you stretch the hide and scrape off the flesh and fat. However, you can simply stretch the fur over the stretcher with the fur inside and tack the skin smooth. Scrape the flesh and fat off the hide carefully. You will get more money for the pelt if it is thoroughly fleshed. Be sure you stretch out and tack the boned and cleaned out tail.

Chapter Ten

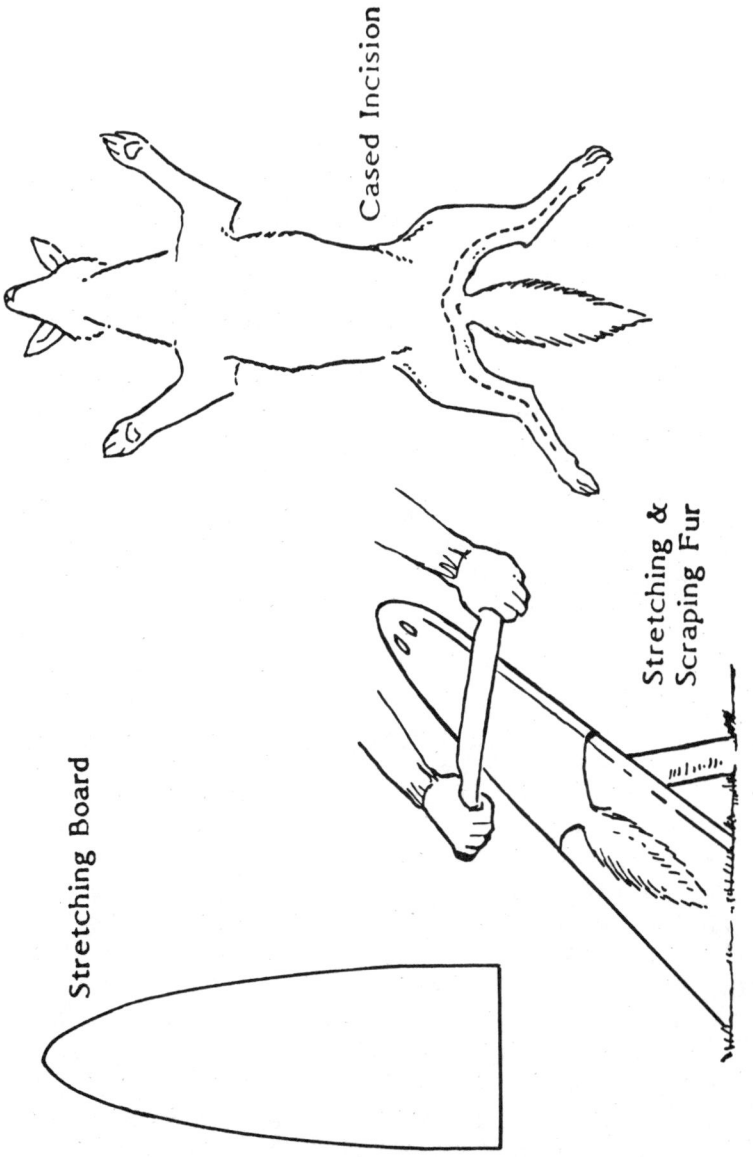

Small Game

Put the stretched skin in a cool, shady, airy place to dry.

WEASEL (ERMINE)
The weasel is an American carnivore having a long, slender body, and feeding largely on small rodents. He is reputed to be the greatest fighter, pound for pound and inch for inch, in the animal kingdom. He will attack a man if he is cornered. At maturity, he is about 13 to 16 inches long.

The ermine is really a weasel with his white winter coat. The fur is expensive and much in demand.

The fur of the weasel or the ermine is cased, fleshed, and stretched as described above. His stretching board is about 15 inches long, 3 inches at the base and 2 inches at the shoulder.

I would appreciate information on gland removal for cleaning and cooking.

MARTEN
The marten is a slender carnivore, usually dark brown in color, who grows two to two and a half feet long at maturity. A well-prepared marten fur is very valuable. His stretcher is 2 feet long, 5 inches wide at the base and 3 inches wide at the shoulder. His fur is cased, fleshed and stretched as described above.

Please send gland removal instructions for cleaning if you have them.

FISHER
The fisher is a dark brown or blackish, foxlike marten. He catches fish for his food. At maturity he is about 3 feet long.

His fur is cased, fleshed and stretched as described above. His stretcher board should be 4 feet long, 10 inches wide at the base and 5 inches wide at the shoul-

Chapter Ten

der.

I would appreciate gland removal information for cleaning.

FOX

The fox is a carnivore of the dog family. He is characterized by a pointed muzzle, erect ears and a long, bushy tail. He can grow to 3½ feet long and stand over a foot tall.

The fox's track is a combination of the cat's and the dog's. The fox walks, however, almost daintily, the toes widely spaced, and the claws are clearly visible. He sometimes leaves long, narrow holes in the snow where he digs for insects.

His fur is cased, fleshed and stretched as directed above. His stretcher board is 4 feet long, 8 inches wide at the base and 5 inches wide at the shoulder.

Fox Tracks

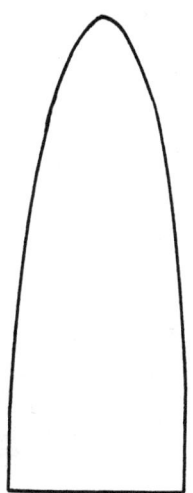

Stretching Board

Small Game

OTTER

The otter is an aquatic, fur-bearing, carnivorous, musteline mammal, with webbed feet and a long, slightly flattened tail. It can attain 3½ feet in length and a foot in height. He is the clown of the animal world. He loves to slide down mud banks and plays many games.

His fur is cased, fleshed and stretched as indicated above. His stretcher board should be about 45 inches long, about 8 inches wide at the bottom and about 6 inches wide at the shoulders.

SKUNK

The skunk is a small, striped, fur-bearing, bushy tailed mammal of the weasel family. As a child, we all dreaded skunk trapping time, because some of the boys came to school reeking of their catch. Occasionally they had to be sent home, which they really didn't seem to mind - they could go out and catch more skunks.

The skunk leaves flatfooted, oddly diagonal tracks in the snow, with hardly any hind tracks registering. He is also apt to leave little, round holes in either the snow or turf, where he digs for insects. He is the boldest of the animals because he has confidence in his smelly protection.

Skunk Tracks

Chapter Ten

Skunk meat was a favorite item on the menu for both American Indians and some Mexican Indians. It was sometimes used for medicine, but don't ask me what it cured. Probably a stuffy nose. At any rate, if the scent glands on either side of the rectum are removed without piercing, the meat is said to be superior to chicken. Follow any of the recipes given for small game.

The fur is cased, stretched and fleshed as indicated. The stretcher board should be about 30 inches long, 8 inches wide at the bottom and 4 inches wide at the shoulders.

LYNX, WILDCAT

The lynx is a wild cat with long limbs and a short tail and, usually, tufted ears. It is extremely rare where I live, but the few skins I have seen were very beautiful.

Cat Tracks
(Lynx)

Small Game

The wildcat is a feline said to be widely distributed around the world. I have heard their eerie cry in the woods, and I have friends who had one set up housekeeping in their cellar, but I have not seen one.

The fur of both these animals is cased, fleshed and stretched as indicated above. Their stretcher boards should be about 4 feet long, about 10 inches wide at the base and about 6 inches wide at the shoulders.

The Indians were said to treasure their meat, but nowhere can I find cleaning directions, and I know of no one who has cooked one. I even tried to chase down a man in Cody, Wyoming, who was known to prepare them, but I didn't find him. My response to this is HELP. If anyone has directions on cleaning, gland removal and cooking, please write to me in care of the publishing company listed on the front of the book.

Hare & Rabbit
Chapter 11

Hare

ARCTIC HARE, SNOWSHOE HARE, PRAIRIE HARE, WHITE TAILED HARE, BELGIAN HARE

Hares and rabbits are close relatives. The hare differs in that he does not have his young in an underground burrow, he can open his eyes at birth, and is born with a full coat of hair. The North American Jack Rabbit is really a hare. The Belgian Hare and the Cottontail are true rabbits.

Early naturalists used both names when they wrote about rabbits and hares and for cleaning and cooking purposes we will consider them the same. Please consult the next section on rabbit.

Small Game

Rabbit

(COTTONTAIL, BLACK TAILED JACK RABBIT, NORTH AMERICAN JACK RABBIT, BRUSH RABBIT, EASTERN COTTONTAIL, WHITE-TAILED JACK RABBIT.)

HARE OR RABBIT TRACKS

Hare or Rabbit tracks have the small forefeet placed irregularly behind the large hind feet. If he sits, his little, round, puffy tail leaves a track.

Rabbit Tracks

RABBIT SKINNING

If possible, wear rubber gloves. If you have any cuts or abrasions on your hands it is possible to catch tularemia or rabbit fever from skinning a rabbit.

Audrey Jackson of Ivanhoe, California says, "We live in Tulare County where tularemia is very common. Our county advisors have told many rabbit or hare hunters that one of the best warnings of tularemia is white spots on the liver. If any white spots are seen on the liver you should discard it completely because the rabbit is infected. In our area we cannot eat Jack Rabbits at all."

Chapter Eleven

Thank you Audrey. I appreciate the many readers who have added their knowledge to this field.

Rabbit skin is not tough and so it is not one of the more desirable furs. However, it has some commercial value and, after it is stretched, it can be cut into two inch strips and woven into a very soft and warm blanket.

SKINNING IF THE FUR IS TO BE SAVED

Cut along the inside of the hind legs and across the rump at the vent, as shown. This type of skinning is called "casing".

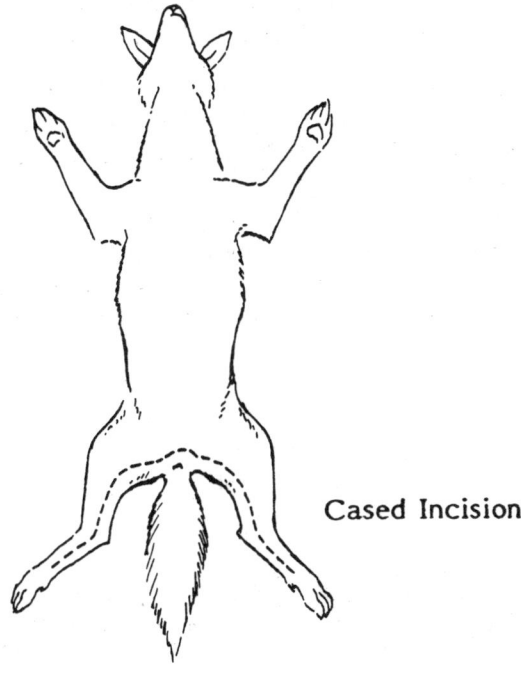

Cased Incision

Small Game

Work out the hind legs and the feet, then pull off the skin inside out as you would remove a glove. If the fur is dirty, wash it with soap and water, then dry it. Stretch it inside out over your stretcher.

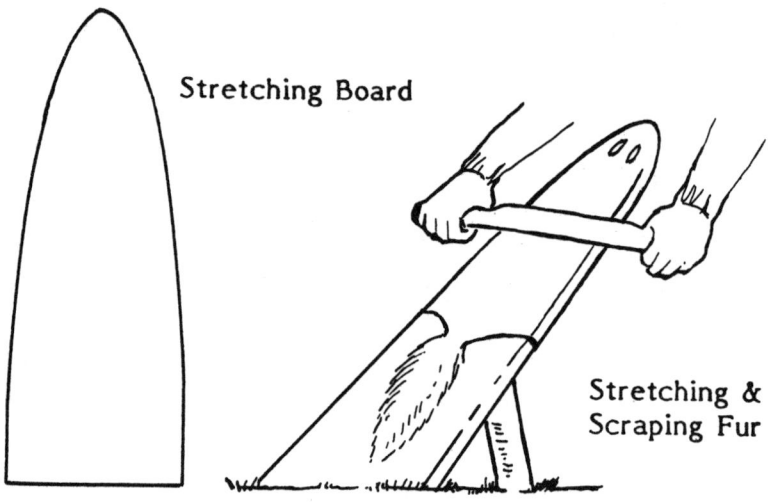

Stretching Board

Stretching & Scraping Fur

Chapter Eleven

The stretcher should be made from boards 1/2 to 3/4 inch thick. Make sure that all edges are rounded and smooth, so you will not tear the fur. It should be about 20 inches long, 4 inches wide at shoulders and 6 inches wide at base.

Scrape all flesh from the inside of the pelt, being very careful not to pierce the skin. Put the stretched fur in a cool, shady place and allow to dry.

SKINNING IF THE FUR IS NOT TO BE SAVED

If you are going to throw the fur away, cut through the skin at the nape of the neck, hold the head with one hand and pull off the skin with the other. The skin is very loose and pulls off easily. If there are any hairs left on the carcass, singe them off over an open flame. Now, wash the meat thoroughly with cold, running water. Make sure all the blood and clots are washed out.

RABBIT CLEANING

If the pelt is not going to be saved, the rabbit should be cleaned in the field. Simply slit the stomach from the neck to the vent and remove the guts.

If you are "casing" the fur you will, of course, have to draw the animal after you skin him, unless you want to remove the guts from the bottom slit.

AGE OF THE RABBIT OR HARE

If the claws of the animal are blunt and ragged and the ears are dry and tough, the rabbit is old. If his claws are smooth and sharp and his ears supple and tender, he is young and tender. A young rabbit or hare may be roasted or fried without braising, but an older one must be braised, that is, cooked slowly and long with added moisture. He may also be presimmered until tender, as in the following recipe.

Small Game

FRIED RABBIT (For the older rabbit)
Cut, skin, singe and wash the rabbit. Cut it into quarters, or smaller pieces if desired. Put it into a deep pot, cover it with cool water and add 1/4 cup vinegar and 1 teaspoon salt. Bring to a boil and simmer for 15 minutes or until fork tender. Drain off the water and toss the rabbit pieces in a paper bag containing 1 cup of flour, 1½ teaspoon salt and 1 teaspoon pepper. Fry out 4 strips of bacon and put it on a paper towel. Add 4 tablespoons butter or margarine to the bacon drippings. Lay the floured rabbit in the bacon drippings and add 1 large onion, thinly sliced. Sauté the rabbit COVERED for 15 minutes, keeping a gentle sizzle. Turn and gently sizzle him for 15 minutes more, COVERED. Put on a warm platter, lay the fried onions over and sprinkle with crumbled bacon.

FRIED RABBIT (For the young animal)
Cut, skin, singe and wash the rabbit. Cut it into serving sized pieces. Sprinkle it with tenderizer, if you have any. Put into a pan 1/2 cup of butter, margarine or bacon drippings. Dip the pieces into one well-beaten egg, then press on bread or cracker crumbs. Place in the sizzling butter, turn the heat low and COVER. Fry very gently for 15 minutes, turn the pieces, COVER and fry for 15 more minutes. Remove to a platter and add to the pan drippings 1 chopped onion. Fry until soft, pour over the rabbit and serve.

POTTED HARE
Cut, skin, singe and wash the hare. Quarter it and put it into a stewpan with 3 pieces of bacon laid over it. Add 2 cups of water, 2 chopped onions, 1 chopped carrot and 1 teaspoonful salt. COVER and simmer gently until it is very tender. (The time will depend on the

age of your hare. It could vary from 1 hour to 3 hours. Add more water or broth if necessary.) Allow it to cool when done.

Pour off the broth, remove the bones from the hare and chop the meat, bacon and vegetables very fine. (A food processor is great for this.) Add salt, pepper, worcestershire sauce, catsup, allspice and cloves to taste. A little sherry may be added if you like the taste. Press the mixture into glass, etc. pots or loaf pans. Pour clarified butter or melted lard or other shortening over it to seal and refrigerate. This may be served cold or hot, in sandwiches or as a main dish.

This recipe is at least a hundred years old and was probably the forerunner of our modern spam.

ROAST RABBIT WITH CREAM GRAVY

Gut, skin, singe and wash rabbit as directed. Dry him and rub him inside and out with gin. Salt and pepper him lightly, inside and out. Put in the cavity 1 orange, cut into 8 pieces, 1 onion cut in eighths and 3 whole cloves. Sew up cavity and put the rabbit in a greased roasting pan. Cover his top with thinly sliced salt pork or bacon. Pour into the pan 1 cup undiluted chicken bouillon and 1/8 cup burgundy or a light, red wine. Add 1 mashed garlic clove, 3 tablespoons gin, 1 small chopped carrot and 1/8 teaspoon salt. Set the pan UNCOVERED in a preheated 450° F. oven for 10 minutes, then lower the heat to 350° F. and roast for 45 minutes more, basting frequently.

Split the rabbit in two lengthwise and lay, belly down, on a warm platter. Discard orange and whole cloves, cover and keep warm. Pour pan drippings and onion from the cavity and 1 tablespoon flour into the blender and liquefy for 5 seconds. Pour into a saucepan, bring to a boil, stirring, and cook gently until thick and bubbling. Taste for seasoning, pour over the

Small Game

rabbit and serve.

HASENPFEFFER
Many recipes have been give for this but I will try to keep it simple.

Gut, skin, singe and wash the rabbit. Cut it into quarters or pieces. Put in a crock and cover it with vinegar and water, in equal parts. Add 1 sliced onion, 1 teaspoon salt, 10 peppercorns, or ½ teaspoon pepper, 1 bay leaf and 1 teaspoon Italian seasoning. Soak it for 2 days in the refrigerator, turning every 12 hours.

Remove the rabbit from the marinade and toss in a bag containing 1 cup flour and 1 teaspoon salt. Put 5 tablespoons butter or margarine in a kettle and gently brown the rabbit on both sides. Pour the marinade into the kettle with the rabbit and add 1 tablespoon brown sugar. Bring to a boil and simmer, COVERED for 1 hour. Put the rabbit on a warm platter and thicken the liquid with a little flour and water mixture. Taste for seasoning, pour over the rabbit and serve.

RECIPE FOR ROAST HARE FROM 1861
INGREDIENTS - Hare, forcemeat, a little milk, butter.

CHOOSING AND TRUSSING - Choose a young hare, which may be known by its smooth and sharp claws, and by the cleft in the lip not being much spread. To be eaten in perfection, it must hang for some time; and, if properly taken care of, it may be kept for several days. It is better to hang without being paunched; but should it be previously emptied, wipe the inside every day, and sprinkle over it a little pepper and ginger, to prevent the musty taste which long keeping in the damp occasions, and which also affects the stuffing. After it is skinned, wash it well, and soak for an hour in warm water to draw out the blood; if old, let it

Chapter Eleven

lie in vinegar for a short time, but wash it well afterwards in several waters. Make a forcemeat (below), wipe the hare dry, fill the belly with it, and sew it up. Bring the hind and forelegs close to the body towards the head, run a skewer through each, fix the head between the shoulders by means of another skewer, and be careful to leave the ears on. Put a string round the body from skewer to skewer, and tie it above the back.

Roast Hare

Small Game

MODE - The hare should be kept at a distance from the fire when it is first laid down, or the outside will become dry and hard before the inside is done. Baste it well with milk for a short time, and afterwards with butter; and particular attention must be paid to the basting, so as to preserve the meat on the back juicy and nutritive. When it is almost roasted enough, flour the hare, and baste well with butter. When nicely frothed, dish it, remove the skewers, and send it to table with a little gravy in the dish, and a tureen of the same. Red-currant jelly must also not be forgotten, as this is an indispensable accompaniment to roast hare. For economy, good beef dripping may be substituted for the milk and butter to baste with; but the basting as we have before stated, must be continued without intermission. If the liver is good, it may be parboiled, minced, and mixed with the stuffing; but it should not be used unless quite fresh.

TIME A middling-sized hare, 1¼ hour; a large hare, 1½ to 2 hours
AVERAGE COST From 4 s. to 6 s. (20¢ to 30¢)
SUFFICIENT FOR 5 or 6 persons
SEASONABLE from September to the end of February

FORCEMEAT STUFFING 2 oz. of ham or lean bacon, ¼ lb. of suet, the rind of half a lemon, 1 teaspoonful of minced parsley, 1 teaspoonful of minced sweet herbs; salt, cayenne, and pounded mace to taste; 6 oz. of breadcrumbs, 2 eggs.

MODE Shred the ham or bacon, chop the suet, lemon-peel and herbs, taking particular care that all be very finely minced; add a seasoning to taste, of salt, cayenne and mace, and blend all thoroughly together with the bread-crumbs, before wetting. Now beat and strain

Chapter Eleven

the eggs, work these up with the other ingredients, and the forcemeat will be ready for use. When it is made into balls, fry of a nice brown, in boiling lard, or put them on a tin and bake for 1/2 hour in a moderate oven. As we have stated before, no one flavour should predominate greatly, and the forcemeat should be of sufficient body to cut with a knife, and yet not dry and heavy. For very delicate forcemeat, it is advisable to pound the ingredients together before binding with the egg; but for ordinary cooking, mincing very finely answers the purpose.

NOTE - In a forcemeat for HARE, the liver of the animal is sometimes added. Boil for 5 minutes, mince it very small, and mix it with the other ingredients. If it should be in an unsound state, it must on no account be made use of.

CARVING THE RABBIT
In carving a boiled rabbit, let the knife be drawn on each side of the backbone, the whole length of the rabbit, as shown by the dotted line 3 to 4: thus the rabbit will be in three parts. Now let the back be divided into two equal parts in the direction of the line from 1 to 2; then let the leg be taken off, as shown by the line 5 to 6, and the shoulder, as shown by the line 7 to 8. This, in our opinion, is the best plan to carve a rabbit, although there are other modes which are preferred by some.

A roast rabbit is rather differently trussed from one that is meant to be boiled; but the carving is nearly similar, as will be seen by the cut. The back should be divided into as many pieces as it will give, and the legs and shoulders can then be disengaged in the same manner as those of the boiled animal.

Small Game

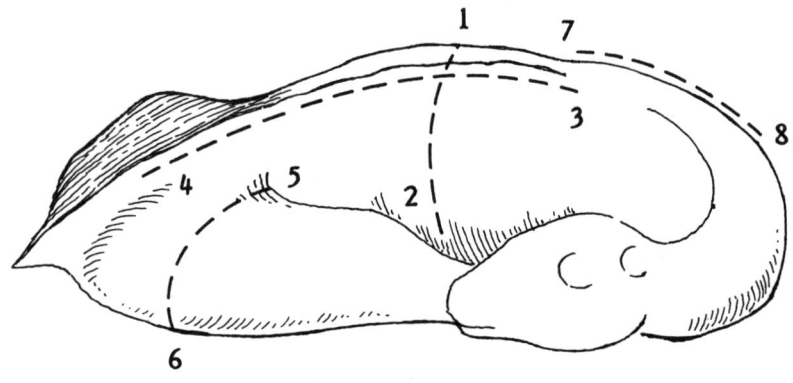

Boiled Rabbit

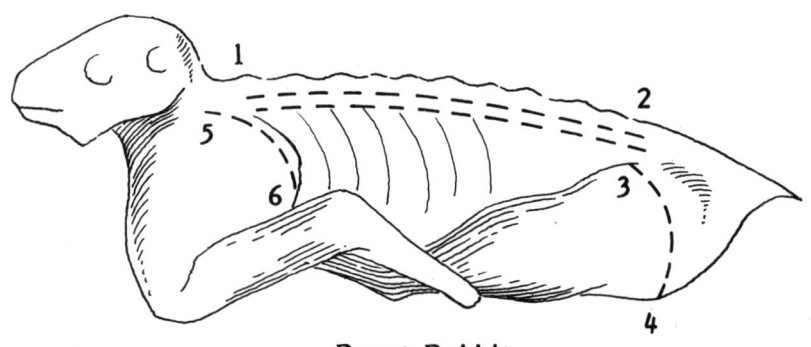

Roast Rabbit

Index

Armadillo	5
Bar-B-Que	6
Cleaning	5
Deviled	7
Beaver	11
Beaver Tail Soup	13
Braised	14
Cleaning	12
Fleshing	12
Marengo	15
Skinning	9
Stretching	12
Tail	13
Tracks	9
Canning	1
Casing	64
Coon - see Raccoon	24
Ermine - see Weasel	66
Explorers Club Menu	Front
Fisher	66
Casing	64, 65
Fleshing	64, 65
Skinning	64, 65
Stretcher Board	66
Fox	67
Casing	64, 65

Index

Fleshing	64, 65	
Skinning	64, 65	
Stretcher Board	67	
Tracks	67	
Groundhog - see Woodchuck	16	
Hare - see Rabbit	72	
Lynx - see Wildcat	69	
Marmot	39	
Baked, with apples	44	
Casing	42	
Cleaning	43	
Curry	45	
Fleshing	43	
Marinated	44	
Skinning to save Fur	40	
Skinning not to save Fur	43	
Stovies	46	
Marten	66	
Casing	64, 65	
Fleshing	64, 65	
Skinning	64, 65	
Stretching Board	66	
Muskrat	47	
Casing	48	
Cleaning	52	
Creole	52	
Fleshing	51	
Fried	54	
Ginned	53	
Skinning to save Fur	48	
Skinning not to save Fur	52	
Stretcher	49	
Tracks	47	
Opossum	56	
Baked	62	
Cased	57	

Index

Cleaning	61
Fleshing	60
Roast	61
Skinning to save hide	57
Skinning not to save hide	61
Tracks	56
Otter	68
Casing	64, 65
Fleshing	64, 65
Skinning	64, 65
Stretcher Board	68
Pickling	3
Possum - see Opossum	56
Rabbit	72
Age	75
Carving	81
Cleaning	75
Fried	76
Hasenpfeffer	78
Potted	76
Roast	77
Roast 1861	78
Skinning to save Fur	72-75
Skinning not to save Fur	72, 75
Tracks	72
Raccoon	24
Age	24
Cleaning	28
Roast	28
Skinning to save Fur	26
Skinning not to save Fur	28
Stretcher	27
Sweet Potatoes & Pineapple	29
Tracks	25
Salting	2
Skunk	68

Index

Casing	64, 65
Fleshing	64, 65
Stretching Board	68
Tracks	68
Smoking	4
Squirrel	31
Casing	33, 34
Cleaning	35
Cooking	35-38
Fleshing	34
Fried	35
Heads	37
Skinning to save Fur	32
Skinning not to save Fur	35
Stew	36
Stretching Pelts	32-34
Tracks	31
Virginia Opossum - see Possum	56
Weasel	66
Casing	64, 65
Fleshing	64, 65
Skinning	64, 65
Stretching Board	66
Whistle Pig - see Woodchuck	16
Whistler of the Rockies - see Marmot	39
Wildcat	69
Casing	64, 65
Fleshing	64, 65
Skinning	64, 65
Stretching Board	70
Woodchuck, Whistle Pig	16
Braised	22
Cased	17
Cleaning	21
Pie	21
Rawhide from	19

Index

Skinning to save Skin	17
Skinning not to save Skin	21
Stretcher	18
Tracks	16

What a Gift!

If you know anyone who hunts or fishes, they'd probably love a copy of these books. Share with them the mouth-watering recipes and simple cleaning instructions for all types of game, fish and fowl. It makes an inexpensive and thoughtful gift.

Simply fill in the coupon below and enclose a check or money order for $9.95 (+ $1.00 postage and handling). We'll send a copy to you in a matter of weeks.

Please send me The Complete Encyclopedia of Wild Game & Fish Cleaning & Cooking. I'm enclosing $9.95 for each 3 volume set I order, plus $1.00 postage and handling.
PA residents add 6% sales tax.

Amount Enclosed .... # of Book Sets ....
Send to: Yesnaby Publishers, RD 8, Box 213, Danville PA 17821

Name _____
Address _____
City _____
State _____ Zip _____